John Corson Smith

History of freemasonry in the city of Galena, Illinois

John Corson Smith

History of freemasonry in the city of Galena, Illinois

ISBN/EAN: 9783337276409

Printed in Europe, USA, Canada, Australia, Japan

Cover: Foto ©Andreas Hilbeck / pixelio.de

More available books at **www.hansebooks.com**

HISTORY OF FREEMASONRY

IN THE

CITY OF GALENA,

ILLINOIS,

FROM THE ORGANIZATION OF

Strangers' Union Lodge No. 14,

A. D. 1826, A. L. 1826,

TO

July A. D. 1874, A. L. 5874,

AND

BY-LAWS

OF

MINERS' LODGE No. 273, A. F. and A. M.
JO DAVIESS CHAPTER No. 51, R. A. M'S.
ELY S. PARKER COUNCIL No. 60, R. S. E. and S. M'S.
GALENA COMMANDERY No. 40, KNIGHTS TEMPLARS.

GALENA:
GAZETTE BOOK AND JOB PRINTING HOUSE,
1874.

TO

THE BRETHREN OF MINERS' LODGE NO. 273,

WITH WHOM SO MANY PLEASANT HOURS HAVE BEEN SPENT IN THE STUDY

OF THE NOBLE SCIENCE OF ANCIENT CRAFT MASONRY, AND THE

APPLICATION OF THOSE THREE PRECIOUS JEWELS

OF THE MASTER MASON, " FRIENDSHIP,

MORALITY AND BROTHERLY

LOVE,"

THE BRETHREN TO WHOSE PARTIALITY

THE AUTHOR HAS BEEN SO OFTEN INDEBTED FOR DISTINGUISHED HONORS,

AND BY WHOM HE HAS BEEN SO "OFT HONORED WITH SUPREME

COMMAND," IS THIS WORK FRATERNALLY DEDICATED.

BY

JOHN C. SMITH, W. M.

THE importance of compiling the history of Masonry in Galena, that the names of our early Masonic workers may be preserved to the Craft, has often been suggested by the members of Miners' Lodge No. 273. No more fitting time has presented itself than the present, when new by-laws were to be published by at least three of the four Masonic bodies in this city, and by combining all the codes in one book, the expense of a separate publication is avoided, and the work bound in a form which will insure its preservation.

The value of such a record cannot be too highly estimated, embracing as it does, the names of many of the earliest and most prominent settlers of the mining regions, active alike in Masonry as they were in all the public measures of the day.

The difficulties attending the writing of this history will be better understood when it is known that the first Lodge—" Strangers' Union "—was organized before the arrival of the U. S. Agent, Capt. Martin Thomas, who came to take charge of the mineral lands on behalf of the Government and to lay out the " village " of Galena, two years before the publication of the first newspaper in this the Northwest.

If the Masonic record be incomplete, the brethren
will bear in mind that it is owing to three reasons:
First, there are no records preserved of the early
meetings of Strangers' Union Lodge No. 14. Second,
we have no knowledge that any member of the old
Lodge is living at the present day. Third, there was
no newspaper published in the lead region at that
time to whose files we may refer for a record of the
event.

CHAPTER I.

The "History of Masonry in Illinois," written by
authority of the Grand Lodge, makes no mention of
a Lodge in Galena until the presenting of a petition
to the Grand Lodge of Missouri Dec. 26th, 1838,
praying that a charter be granted to the "Far West
Lodge."

The historian, Bro. John C. Reynolds, did all in
his power to get a complete record of the Lodges
chartered by the old Grand Lodge of Illinois, which
became defunct in 1829, but, owing to carelessness in
keeping records of Lodges, and the destruction of the
Archives of the Grand Lodge by fire, many important
facts connected with the early history of Masonry in
this State have been lost to the Craft; and for the
same reason the Craft in this city are unable to fix
the date of the organization of their first Lodge.

"Strangers' Union No. 14" was the first Lodge
constituted north of Fulton County and west of Lake

Michigan, and was regularly at work in 1826, having
been authorized at the January session of the Grand
Lodge of Illinois, held in the State House in the town
of Vandalia. From that veteran craftsman, Bro.
P. M. and Sir Knight, Capt. H. H. Gear, we learn
that the names of the first officers of this Lodge were
BRO. LERMON PARKER, W. M.; BRO. MOSES MEEKER,
S. W.; BRO. BENSON HUNT, J. W.; BRO. L. P.
VAUSBURG, Treas. and BRO. JAMES HARRIS, Sec.,
and that his brother Charles Gear was present in
1826, when it was constituted. The most laborious
research of papers and enquiries of the only living
Masons, Bros. H H. Gear and C. C. P. Hunt, who
appear of record as frequent visitors in 1827, fail to
give the desired information as to when this Lodge
was organized.

The first authentic record of "Strangers' Union
Lodge No. 14" bears date April 21st, 1827, and is
as follows:

GALENA, April 21st, A. L. 5827.
    "Strangers' Union Lodge No. 14 met pursuant to adjournment. Mem-
bers present. Chas. Gear, W. M.; James Harris, S. W *pro. tem.;* Benson
Hunt, J. W.; L. P. Vausburg, Treas : G. W. Britton, Sec. ; M. Meeker,
S. D.; M. Faucette, J. D.; W. Spear, Tyler, and Bro. Daniel Moore.
    On motion of Bro. Harris:
Resolved, That the sum of ten dollars be paid for the first or Entered
Apprentice degree, five dollars for the Fellow Craft degree, and ten dol-
lars for the Master Mason degree.
    Bro Sec. presented the petition of John J. Chandler, which was read
and referred to a Committee of Bros. Meeker. Harris and Vausburg.
    On motion of Bro. Harris:
Resolved, That Bro. Meeker be authorized to procure a suitable Lodge
room.
    On motion of Bro. Harris:
Resolved, That the regular communication of this Lodge be held on the
Thursday on or preceeding the full moon in each month.
    On motion of Bro. Harris:
Resolved, That Bro. Sec. be authorized to procure necessary stationery
for the Lodge.
    On motion of Bro. Britton:

Resolved. That a committee of three be appointed to examine petitions and applications for membership.
Bros. Harris, Hunt and Vansburg were appointed the committee.
On motion of Bro Britton:
Resolved, That a committee of three be appointed to revise our By-Laws, and report amendments at our next regular communication.
Bros. C. Gear, M. Meeker and G. W. Britton were appointed the committee.
Lodge closed in harmony."

This is the first record we find of a regular chartered Lodge. The motions to fix the fees for degrees, time of meeting, and rent a suitable room to meet in, would seem to indicate that the Lodge had been but recently organized, but the last motion, " that a committee be appointed to revise our By-Laws and report amendments," taken with the statement of Bro. H. H. Gear, " we had no regular place of meeting. The Lodge was poor and rents high," are satisfactory proof to us that this Lodge was at work as early as 1826.

No later record of the old Grand Lodge of Illinois has been found than January 10th, 1826, at which session charters were granted to Illion Lodge No. 12 and Frontier Lodge No. 13. The latter at Lewiston, Fulton County. In Bro. Reynolds' history of " Masonry in Illinois," we find two more Lodges recorded, Nos. 14 and 15. The former named " La-Fayette," the latter " Sangamon ; " locations unknown. This statement is incorrect, as the records of the session of January, 1826, show that charters were granted to Nos. 12 and 13, and no subsequent record having been found there can be no doubt that No. 14 was our Galena Lodge " Strangers' Union," for which a dispensation may have been granted in said ses-

sion, as charters are not granted until the ability of
the officers and brethren to do good and true Masonic work has been fully tested. We are more in-
clined, however, to believe that a regular charter was
granted at this session from the fact that the No. "14"
is borne upon all the records of "Strangers' Union
Lodge."

The absence of any later record of the "Old"
Grand Lodge of Illinois, the loss by fire in the building of the Galena Branch of the State Bank of Illinois
of the charter, early records and papers of "Strangers' Union" Lodge, and the change in officers from
those named by Bro. Capt. H. H. Gear, which properly took place in December, 1826, are satisfactory
evidence that the banner of Ancient Craft Masonry
was first unfurled and the fires kindled upon its alter
in the city of Galena as early as the summer of 1826.

The next regular communication was held May
11th, when we find recorded the names of two visitors who have since taken an active part in the affairs
of this city, one of whom, Dr. A. T. Crow, has passed
the "Grand Tyler" and been admitted in the Grand
Lodge above. The other is still an honored brother
among us, Capt. H. H. Gear.

Mr. John J. Chandler was made an E. A. A resolution was adopted admitting any brother to membership who "assisted at the instituting of the Lodge"
on the payment of one dollar and fifty cents, the cost
to the original members. These meetings were held
in the month of June. Several petitions were acted

upon and work done in the E. A. degree. Bro. Dr.
A. Philleo, for many years afterward a prominent
citizen, appears as a visitor. Officers were elected on
the 23d as follows: Chas. Gear, W. M.; Benson
Hunt, S. W.; Jas. Smith, J. W.; James Harris,
Treas.; Joseph Hardy, Sec.

One meeting was held in July and another committee appointed " to secure a proper Lodge room."

Aug. 2d.—Lodge met. Officers installed and several brothers elected on demit. A curious custom
prevailed as appears from these old records, of sus-
pending sections 18 and 21 of their by-laws, that a
ballot might be spread upon petitions the night of
presentation. This was a clear violation of one of the
" old regulations " approved St. John the Baptist's
day, 1721, which reads thus: " No man can be accepted a member of a particular Lodge without previous notice *one month before given to the Lodge*, in
order to make due enquiry into the reputation and
capacity of the candidate, *unless by a Dispensation*."

By-Laws were also suspended for the purpose of
Passing and Raising, without having first passed an
examination as to proficiency in Masonic knowledge.
This also was improper and in violation of old regula-
tions. Yet good and true men were these old Masons
coming together from every locality in the mining
region, their Master from the upper waters of "Fevre"
River near Shullsburg, and many from Mineral Point,
Platteville and Dubuque, Wisconsin " Territory,"
Elizabeth, Savanna and other distant points in our

own State, all actuated by the same earnest love of Masonry which has distinguished its votaries from time immemorial.

The next communication was in October, when we find the name of another brother recorded as a visitor, Dr. H. Newhall, since deceased. A man and a Mason long and well known for his active labors in the cause of humanity, a skillful physician and a practical philanthropist, Bro. Newhall joined this Lodge on demit, and for many years was an active member of the Masonic fraternity. Two of his sons have received light in Miners' Lodge No. 273, and found companionship in Jo Daviess Chapter No. 51. Israel Mitchell was iniated.

November 1st, Bro. John J. Chandler, the first initiate of the Lodge, was Passed and Raised. Two other meetings for general work were held during the month.

December 16th and 27th, Lodge met and did work in the E. A. degree. At the latter meeting, T. B. Farnsworth, a brother long an active member of all subsequent Lodges in this city, was initiated.

January 31st, A. L. 5828 three brothers were Passed, one of whom was Bro. Farnsworth. At the meetings in March and April the work was of a general character and in the several degrees.

May 29th an election of officers was had, resulting as follows: Moses Meeker, W. M.; Daniel Murphy, S. W.; M. Faucette, J. W.; Jas. Harris, Treas.; J. J. Chandler, Sec. These officers were initiated June

3d, and the following appointments made: Bro. F. S. Clopton, S. D.; Bro. R. R. Holmes, J. D. A committee was appointed to " procure a suitable room for our next regular communication." This committee failing to report, another one was appointed July 24th, with orders to rent for " four months or a year!"

Evidence of prosperity is here indicated in the presentation of three petitions: One from J. H. Rountree, since a prominent citizen of Wisconsin. And the Craft were fully justified in their desperation to incur so great a liability as the renting of a room for *four months*, or even *one year*.

The W. M., Moses Meeker, presented his bill of $96.24, money paid out for the Craft, which on motion of P. M. Chas. Gear, was ordered paid " out of money not otherwise appropriated."

Now as special orders had been drawn for almost every article which could have been desired or required for the work of the Lodge, we may reasonably infer that this sum of money was for " refreshments " had at the recent installation. Further evidence of prosperous times is found in the order to print 200 copies of the By-Laws, by Mr. Jones, for which they paid the sum of $25. Here is the first record of a Printing Office in Galena.

Records of this meeting are attested by Moses Meeker W M., and J. J. Chandler, Sec.

From July until Dec. the records are missing. Sunday Dec. 1st, a Lodge of sorrow was held and preparations made to attend the funeral of Bro.

Thos. H. January. Officers all present except treasurer, which office Bro., H. Newhall was called upon
to fill and Bro., A. Philleo that of S. D.

All arrangements being perfected, the Lodge adjourned until Monday, Dec., 1st, at 9 o'clock A. M.

The records of this meeting exhibit so fully the
spirit of Masonry as exemplified by the brethren of
"Strangers' Union Lodge" that we give them in
full:

"MONDAY, Dec. 2d, A. L. 5828, 9 o'clock.
" Lodge met pursuant to adjournment.
" The Lodge then proceeded to take charge of the funeral of Bro.
Thos. H. January, who was buried according to the Ancient Masonic
custom.
"Visiting Brethren—Abner Fields, A. T. Crow, H. H. Gear, Jas.
Douglass, of Davis Lodge No. 22, Lexington, —— Woodbridge, L. Frank-
lin, Union Lodge No 7, Mo., and Morris Holmes, of Morning Lodge,
Albany.
"Moved and seconded, that a committee of five be appointed to remove
the body of our deceased brother's wife to the place of his interment.
The following were the committee: Bros. A. T. Crow, A. Philleo, Jas.
Harris, Abner Fields and M. Faucette.
" Lodge closed in Harmony.
" J. J. CHANDLER, Sec.   " M. MEEKER, Master.'

We regret that the Secretary forgot that good Masonic usuage, which requires that the names of all the
brethern present be recorded, as there is no doubt
but there was a large attendance; and that this was
the first funeral in the great north-west where the
solemn and beautiful rites of Free Masonary were observed.

December 13th, the W. M. read an address relative
to the propriety of surrendering the charter. On motion it was resolved, "that the charter be retained
and G. L. dues paid for 1827-8."

The usual committee was appointed "to procure a
suitable Lodge room."

December 20th, Brother Fields, Harris and Gear,

were appointed a committee "to make arrangements for celebrating the 27th, by providing a dinner, and *obliging* some brother to deliver an address."

Here is how they celebrated "Saturday December 27th, A. L. 5828."

"Lodge met pursuant to adjournment, when the brethren proceeded to celebrate this day in due and ancient form.

"On motion of Bro. Chandler and seconded by Bro. Hunt, that Bros. A and B be not permitted to walk in procession to-day. Carried by a unanimous vote of the Lodge."

The Lodge then proceeded to celebrate the day (parade we presume,) and then adjourned until 6 o'clock P. M., when it again convened pursuant to adjournment.

"On motion the 21st section of the By-Laws was dispensed with for the time being. Bro. Sec. presented and read the petition of Benjamin Dolrey for Masonry. Referred to a committee of Bros. Murphy, Harris and Hunt.

"The Lodge was then opened in the 2d degree and proceeded to confer the F. C. degree upon Bros. Barrel and Morse.

"Bro. Sec. presented and read the petition of D. B. Morehouse for Masonry, which was referred to a committee of Bros. Holmes, Hunt and Chandler

"On motion, Bros Chandler, Holmes and Faucetle were appointed a committee to get Bro. Chas. Gear to lecture from day to day, until the brethren had made such advance as would enable them to work.

"Visiting brethren—Bros. Abner Fields, Jas Clark, Charles C. P. Hunt, H. H. Gear, Jonathan Brown, Culver Woodburn, A. Philleo, H. Newhall, Eliot Kerney, Philip Rosebrough, of Western Star Lodge No. 1, Kaskaskia, Thos. Moore, Edon Lodge No. 11, and Robt, Adams, of Union Lodge No. 7.

"Lodge closed in Harmony."

Our curiosity being excited to know why those two bros. "A" and "B" were "not permitted to walk in the procession" we have made repeated enquiries of Bros. H. H. Gear and C. C. P. Hunt, but they have as steadily refused, and ask the indulgence of the Craft for the refusal, pleading that they were the guests of Strangers' Union Lodge on that occasion, and that it would be improper and discourteous to disclose anything which took place during that "celebration in due and ancient form, Dec. 27th, 1828."

Remembering the social customs of those early days, from which not even our fraternity was exempt and the fact, that Galena was a frontier town, outside the pale fall of civlization, we submit, that the brethren were excusable for being tired so early in the day, and thus getting excused from joining in the procession.

January 2nd, A. L. 5829.—D. B. Morehouse for many years so well known as Captain Morehouse was initiated. Brother Morehouse took an active part in Masonry until his death in 1870, holding membership at that time in Miner's Lodge No. 273 and Jo Daviess Chapter No. 51.

On the 3rd inst., Brother T. B. Farnsworth, also a member of the above named Lodge and Chapter at the time of his death, was raised to the sublime degree of Master Mason.

Here occurs a period of unusal prosperity and press of work reminding the brethern of Miner's Lodge of the charge so often made, that they frequently work "eight nights in the week." To this we may plead guilty, with this qualification, that we do not, never have, and never will do other work on the Sabbath, than that of a Lodge of sorrow. Our brethern of Strangers' Union Lodge did not however hesitate to do general work, and confer degrees on the Sabbath, and we for one say, they were excusable. Situated as they were at that early day, we doubt if there was any more proper place, in which our brethren could congregate, or more durable work in which to engage than that to be found in the work of a Masonic Lodge.

January 4th, the Lodge was in session and on the 7th, Brother James Craig was elected on demit.

Sunday 11th, Brother Morehouse, Crafted.

12th, Brother Morse Raised.

13th, Brother Block Crafted. Many visitors were present, among whom was Bro. Samuel Smoker, of Philanthropic Lodge, No. 104, who afterwards became a member on demit. A petition was received from Mr. William Hempstead, an active business man and prominent citizen, whose generous liberality as a Mason, during the remainder of his life, only equaled by his love for the church with which he was connected.

Jan. 14th, Wm. Hempstead elected and initiated.

Jan. 16th, Bro. E. Black raised.

Jan. 17th, Bro. D. B. Morehouse raised.

Jan. 31st, work in E. A. degree, and Bro. Newhall joined on demit.

Sunday, Feb. 1st, Bro. Wm. Hempstead crafted.

Feb. 14th and 15th, Lodge met for work in E. A. and F. C. degrees. From this time Bro. James Craig became the Secretary, and the minutes show much care and are beautifully written. Bro. Craig afterwards settled in Wappelo, now Hanover, where he died honored by all who knew him.

March 14th and 21st, work in all of the degrees. Bro. J. H. Rountree raised.

March 22d, Bros. Wm. Hempstead and Peter Prim were examined in open Lodge as to their proficiency in the first two degrees of Masonry, which proved satisfactory. This is the first record we have of an examination. Bros. Hempstead and Prim were then raised to the sublime degree of Master Mason.

March 27th, Lodge met and arranged to inter Bro. F. S. Clopton with Masonic honors.

March 30th, work on E. A. degree.

April 18th, we find an order of $8.00 drawn in favor of Bro. Wm. Hempstead to pay for "music at funeral of Bro. F. S. Clopton," also the following good thing, which is a contract with the Tyler, defining his duties and emoluments: "The committee appointed to procure a Tyler, reported that Bro. James Harris would accept the station and perform the duties on the following terms: One dollar for each meeting, 50 cents for summoning the members in town to special meetings and serving process from the Lodge, the same fees as the sheriff is allowed for serving summons. His duties will be to tile the Lodge, keep the room in order, have wood and candles supplied at the expense of the Lodge, and when the clothing wants washing, he is to procure it done the Lodge to pay on his order for the same."

May 14th, Lodge met for general work.

June 11th, A. L. 5829, A. D. 1829.—At this communication of the Lodge, a resolution was adopted postponing the election of officers, and agreeing that *all* the officers should hold over. This is no doubt one of the main causes why the Lodge soon ceased to work, which it certainly did, no more records of its meetings being found. When the brethren of a Lodge arrive at the conclusion that they cannot make *any* change in their officers, they are then as certain to destroy their Lodge as a brother is to destroy his usefulness when he believes the Lodge cannot exist without his services. The next worst thing to re-electing the same officers year after year, is to have them " hold over," and the Masonic body which will do this must sooner or later surrender its charter. This resolution was offered:

"*Resolved*, That we return our charter to the G. M. or D. G. M. of Illinois, and apply to the G. L. of Missouri for a new one."

The further consideration of this question was postponed until the 18th inst.

The strictest search and most diligent enquiry fail to give any further light upon the doings of "Strangers' Union Lodge." Whether it died because of failure to hold the annual election; because the G. L. of Illinois had become defunct, or because of the storm of fanaticism which was then abroad in the land, we cannot tell. Perhaps it was all three combined. Suffice it to say, that Galena was not long without a Masonic Lodge. But we anticipate we have been thus full in our history of " Strangers' Union Lodge No. 14," the first Lodge in the " North West" that the brethren of Miners' Lodge should know to whom they were indebted for the early introduction of Masonry in this frontier town. To complete this record, we give the names of all borne upon the records as members, the names of all who were Initiated, Passed or Raised, together with the names and address of all visitors, so far as recorded:

MEMBERS NAMES.

Lemon Parker,	Charles Gear,	James Harris,
Benson Hunt,	L. P. Vausburg,	Moses Meeker,
M. Faucette,	W. Spear.	G. W. Britton,
Daniel Moore,	— Clayne,	James Smith,
Thos. H. January,	Jos. Hardy,	R. R. Holmes,
Alben T. Crow,	Jas. A. Clark,	John O. Hancock
John Colter,	W. F. Maneyen,	F. S. Clopton,
James Craig,	Saml. Smoker,	E. Welch,
	Horatio Newhall.	

INITIATED.

R. P. Guyard,   Saml. Jamison,   J. R. Vineyard. Jesse B. Williams, J. P. B. Gratiot.

INITIATED AND PASSED.

A. C. Caldwell,   Israel Mitchell,   John Barrell, Lieut. Christopher, C. Hobert, U. S. A.

INITIATED, PASSED AND RAISED.

John J. Chandler,   E. Block,   Danl. Murphy, T. B. Farnsworth,   J. R. Hammett Peter Prim, L. R. M. Morse,   D. B. Morehouse Wm. Hempstead J. H. Rountree.

VISITORS.

Capt. H. H. Gear,	L. Hadley,	Gov. John Wood,
Benj. Burbridge,	— Swallow,	John Johnson,
A. Philleo,	Kenaly Friar,	E. Brigham,

— Blanchard,   N. F. Smith, Geo. Hackett,

M. Smith,   Jas. Wanton, — Holman,

Robt. Clark,   — Massey,   J. S. Parker,

T. Jones,   J. Bivins,   Douglass Bailey.

Alsworth Baker, — Woodbridge.

Morris Holmes, Morning Lodge, Albany.

H. P. Rundle, Olive Branch Lodge No. 4.

Jonathan Brown, Olive Branch Lodge No. 4.

John Campbell, Maysville Lodge No. 26, Ky.

Elliot Kerney, Equality Lodge No. 136.

— Bowling, Mystic Lodge No. 74.

N. F. Dean, Zion Lodge, Detroit.

Chas. C. P. Hunt, Detroit Lodge, Detroit.

Philip Rochblane, Western Star Lodge No. 1, Illinois.

Thos. Moore, Edon Lodge No. 11.

Robt. Adams, Union Lodge No. 7, Missouri.

James Barnes, Ciota Lodge No. 6.

Wm. Bennett, Edon Lodge No. 11.

Seleh Beach, St. John's Lodge No. 8.

Jas. Reynolds, Hebron Lodge No. 18.

Wm. M. Penn, E. A., Lebanon Lodge, Tenn.

P. Hinney, Mt. Zion Lodge No. 9. Knox Co., Ohio.

J. R. Carter, Abraham Lodge No. 7, Louisville, Kentucky.

Jas. Douglass, Davis Lodge No. 22, Lexington.

L. Franklin, Union Lodge No. 7, Missouri.

Francis Allon, Warren Lodge No. 23.

Belus Jones, La Fayette Lodge No. 14.

Jas. Nagle, Olive Branch Lodge No. 4.

Samuel Phillips, Adair City Lodge No. 27, Ky.

Hampton Wade, La Fayette Lodge No. 14.

John T. Potter, St. Louis Lodge No. 1.

Culver Woodburn, Olive Branch Lodge No. 4.

Wm. Richards, N. C. Harmony Lodge No. 2, Cincinnati, Ohio.

Daniel Mclelain, Hiland Lodge No. 28, Hillsboro, Ohio.

Ephraim F. Ogden, Cincinnati Lodge No. 17, N. J.

Able Proctor, Richmond Lodge No. 10, Va.

Loran Wheeler, Elan Lodge No. 12.

W. J. Freeland, Missouri Lodge No. 1.

J. E. Woolcot, Clinton Lodge No. 143.

H. Beash, Cincinnati Lodge No. 17, N. J.

Abner Fields, Union Lodge No. 10.

Galena Lodge U. D.

A. L. 5830.

Far West Lodge U. D. and No. 29,

Under the M. W. Grand Lodge of Missouri; Dec. 29th, A. L
5838, to June 26th, A. L. 5846.

Far West Lodge No. 5 and No. 41,

Under the M. W. Grand Lodge of Illinois, June 29th, A. L.
5846, to Sept. 1st, A. L. 5848.

Galena Lodge U. D.

Under the M. W. Grand Lodge of Wisconsin, A. L. 5846.

Phœnix Lodge U. D.

Under the M. W. Grand Lodge of Illinois; February A. L.
5854, to March A. L. 5855.

GALENA LODGE U. D.

Our last chapter closes with the motion pending to surrender the Charter of " Strangers' Union Lodge No. 4." No later record can be found, and as the Grand Lodge of Illinois had ceased its existence, so did this and all other subordinate Lodges in the State.

The first record of Galena Lodge U. D. states that it is working under a Dispensation from the Grand Lodge of Missouri. The date of this record is July 17th, A. L. 5830:

"Officers and members present, Bro. Benjamin Mills, W. M.; Daniel Wann, S. W.; Moses Meeker, J. W. p. t.; Wm. Hempstead, S. D.; Samuel Smoker, Sec.

"Visitors.—Bros. Jas. A. Clark, Jas. Barns and Lewis M. Morse.

"Lodge opened in the third degree. Committee on by-laws reported, and report recommitted."

The next meeting is on the 22d, and is entirely taken up with business on by-laws. But one other meeting is recorded, and that on the 29th, when a petition for initiation is read and referred, and one for membership on Demit. The name of Bro. T. B. Farnsworth appears as J. D.

This is the brief history—all which can be found—of Galena Lodge U. D., working under Dispensation

from the Grand Lodge of Missouri. For eight years
and more the Great Lights of Masonry were closed
except in the privacy of the family. The storm of
Anti-Masonic fanaticism had swept over our fair land,
and Masonry in Galena as elsewhere had bowed its
head and waited in silence the return of reason.
During all that period of Masonic darkness, the fraters
of Strangers' Union Lodge never forgot the divine
teachings so often inculcated around its altar, and no
sooner did persecution cease than they hastened to
take steps for the formation of a new Lodge.

FAR WEST LODGE U. D.

December 27th, A. L. 5838, pursuant to a public notice, the following named Master Masons met in the " Chamber of Commerce: "

Chas. Gear,   A. T. Crow,   T. B. Farnsworth,
H. H. Gear,   M. Faucette,   E. W. Turner,
S. McLean,   John Sherman,   John E. Smith,
       R. Pattison and Jas. A. Clark.

These brethren proceeded to organize by electing the following officers:

Chas. Gear, W. M.   E. W. Turner, S. W.
S. McLean, J. W.   T. B. Farnsworth, Treas.
John E. Smith, Sec.   A. T. Crow, S. D.
H. H. Gear, J. D.   M. Faucette, Tyler.

Who were afterwards installed in form, Nov. 16th, 1839, in the stone buildings east side of Main street, opposite Diagonal, then used as a Court House, by P. M. William R. Smith, of Pennsylvania, whose eloquent oration on that pleasing occasion was ordered printed, and 500 copies were distributed among the friends of the craft.

A committee was appointed to draw up a petition

to the G. L. of Missouri for a Dispensation, when
the Lodge adjourned until the 29th. The petition
was drawn up in due form and signed by all present,
and before being forwarded, Bros. Daniel Wann,
George M. Mitchell and Samuel Smoker's names
were added thereto. One well known citizen and
member being prevented from signing by reason of
the following resolution:

"*Resolved*, That owing to the atheistical opinions as publicly expressed
by A B, he is unworthy of being taken by the hand as a Mason."
Which was unanimously adopted.

This is sound Masonic law, and speaks well for
the brethren forming the new Lodge, as it is one of
the old charges which says: "A Mason is obliged
by his tenure to obey the moral law; and if he rightly
understands the Art, he will never be a stupid
atheist, nor an irreligious libertine."

A committee was appointed to procure a room.
Said committee reported January 5th, 1839, when
the brothers subscribed five dollars each toward
fitting up the Lodge.

January 19th, Bro. Daniel Wann, on behalf of the
committee previously appointed to look up the "jewels of the old Lodge," reported their inability to find
any but the S. and J. Wardens columns.

Meetings were held every two weeks until March
23d, when a Dispensation from the Grand Lodge of
Missouri was received, read and accepted. Bro. E.
L. Ogden was thanked for procuring said Dispensation, and admitted free of the regular fee. Bros. C.
P. Burrows and T. C. Legate also became members. From this date commences the work of "Far

West Lodge U. D." afterward No. 29, under the G. L. of Missouri.

Petitions were received from Wm. H. Hooper and A. J. Jackson.

April 6th Wm. H. Hooper and A. J. Jackson were elected and initiated. These gentlemen were well known to all Galenians. The first, since a member of Congress, and the last long the efficient clerk of the city, and but recently deceased. Bro. R. Thompson was admitted to membership. Regular work was continued without anything worthy of special mention until October 18th, when Bro. Geo. M. Mitchell returned from the G. L. of Missouri and presented the Lodge with its Charter as " Far West Lodge No. 29," by which it was hereafter to be known.

March 21st, A. L. 5840.—In answer to a communication from Bodley Lodge No. 1, of Quincy, Ill., relative to the formation of a new Grand Lodge, Bros. James L. James and Dennis Rockwell were appointed as proxies to represent Far West Lodge in the proposed convention to be held at Jacksonville the first Monday in April, and recommended that the G. L. be located at Springfiield.

The Secretary, Bro. John E. Smith, under same date congratulates the Lodge on its prosperous condition as follows :

" Cash receipts,   -   -   - $353 87.

Paid out, -   -   -   -   -   352 75.

Leaving a balance of $1.12¼.

Wonderful prosperity ! Just like " John E." The report continues: " M. M's 27, E. A, 8." There

had been nine initiations and six raisings, which was
a large amount of work for a new Lodge, and the
fact that they were out of debt was to their credit.
The years 1841 and 1842 were prosperous ones for
Far West Lodge. Much interest seems to have
been taken in the meetings, there being a large
attendance of the brethren and visitors. A brief
glance at the latter shows how universal is Masonry.
We find at one meeting as visitors, Gen. George
Cubbage, Iowa Territory, M. Sullivan, Benevolence
Lodge No. 273, England, John S. Crawford, Ballabay
Lodge No. 192, Ireland, Benjamin W. Reney, Har-
mony Lodge, Indiana, Elisha Dwelle, St. Andrew's
Lodge, Boston, Mass., Benedict Solomon, Mechanics
Lodge No. 153, N. Y.

May 16th, 1841.—The petition to the Grand Lodge
of Missouri of " certain Master Masons for a Lodge
to be located at Mineral Point, Wisconsin Territory," was recommended.

July 2d, 1842.—A Lodge of sorrow was held and
resolutions adopted expressive of the feelings of the
brethren on learning of the death of Bro. John
Sherman in Missouri. Bro. G. C. Ehlenfreit Beaner,
Maister of St. Andrew's Lodge No. 388, London,
England, applied for and received relief July 16th.
The death of Bro. Philip S. Dade, of Dubuque, Iowa
Territory, was announced July 22d. Grand Visitor
Alex. T. Douglass, of Missouri, lectured the Lodge
for several days, the brethren being highly pleased
as well as instructed.

August 22d.—The petition of several brother

Master Masons of Dubuque, Iowa Territory, to the
G. L. of Missouri, for Dispensation, was presented,
read, and on motion recommended, also a petition
from divers brethren at Platteville, Wisconsin Territory, for Dispensation, was recommended to the G.
L. of Missouri.

January 14, 1843. In the records of this month we
find the Lodge attended the funeral of Bro. Samuel
Smoker, to whose memory the Secretary, Bro. R.
Pattison, pays this eloquent tribute: " Whilst the
sacred charities of our Noble Order shall be dear to
the Mason's heart, so long shall the recollection of our
deceased brother's manly virtues and goodness, be
present to the surviving brethren of Far West
Lodge." Light be the earth upon his grave.

The records of 1843, '44 and '45, are very imper-
fect, here and there a pencil memorandum from
which we have been able to rescue but a few of the
many interesting facts connected with the history of
this Lodge. We find that after meeting in the Court
House for a year or two, they found comfortable quar-
ters in the commodious stone house on the east side
of the river owned by Bro. John P. DeZoya, where
they met in regular communication during the years
1843-4.

Sunday, March 10th, 1844, the Lodge met to attend
the funeral of Bro. John Turney, Dubuque Lodge
No. 3, of Iowa, and many brethren from abroad participating. This was undoubtedly the largest Masonic funeral which ever took place in this city, Bro.
Turney being universally respected and loved by all

who knew him. The funeral took place from the Episcopal Church, the several Lodges of Odd Fellows participating.

July 17th, we find our brethren called upon again to attend a funeral, that of brother David Wells, which they did in large numbers.

October 3d, all the members were summoned and visitors requested to meet at Lodge room in Bro. John P. DeZoya's. Object of meeting not stated. The following names appear here for the first time. We do not know if they were members of the Lodge or visitors, but give them a place in our record as having been recognized among the old Masons:

Stephen Hempstead, Jas. Douglass, R. J. Depue, A. S. Buchanan, Thos. E. Browne S. E. Lewis, Geo. L. Nightingale, X. Wachtler, P. G. Genes, Wm. Bennett, James Edwards, Sol. Oliver, John Kresse.

Dec. 26th, 1844, the propriety of changing their allegience from the G. L. of Missouri to that of Wisconsin was discussed, and a resolution adopted that "application be formally made to the Grand Lodge of Wisconsin for a Charter, and if granted that the name be that of Galena Lodge. Bro. M. Y. Johnson was elected on Demit, and made Secretary. Nothing of interest appears in the work until March 20th, 1846, when a Lodge of Sorrow convened, to attend the funeral of an old and active member, T. C. Legate.

March 21st, we find what would surprise us did we not know there was such a Lodge: " *Resolved*, That

Bros. Morse and Welch, members of *Galena Lodge*, be admitted free." Which was carried.

The Secretary was then instructed to enquire of the " Grand Secretary of Illinois on what terms a Charter can be procured."

June 22d, 1846, M. W. G. M. Rev. Bro. Wm. F. Walker being present and in the East, the Lodge was opened in " ample form " when it was resolved that " we accept a Charter from the Grand Lodge of Illinois, and return our present Charter to the Grand Lodge of Missouri."

An invitation from Dubuque Lodge No. 3, to participate with them in the celebration of St. John's Day, was accepted, when the Lodge went into an election of officers, with the following result:

M. Y. Johnson, W. M.   W. C. Bostwick, S. W.
Daniel Wann, J. W.   M. P. Silverburgh, Treas.

D. H. Moss, Sec.

June 26th.—Officers installed and appointed:

Osee Welch, S. D.   J. E. Smith, J. D.
P. J. Dennevan, Steward.   Jos. Dopler, Steward.

H. H. Gear, Tyler.

After a brief season spent in lecturing and general work, the M. W. G. M. closed the Lodge in due form until the 26th inst, when the officers elected and appointed were " duly installed and invested with their jewels and badge," the retiring Master, H. H. Gear, delivering a valedictory address, and the new Master, M. Y. Johnson, an inaugural, when Far West Lodge No. 29, under the jurisdiction of the

Grand Lodge of Missouri, closed, never to resume. We deem it fitting to end this chapter with a list of the members and the work of No. 29 so far as completed, omitting the names of those who were only Initiated or Passed. It being well known that no one is recognized as entitled to any Masonic privileges until raised to the sublime degree of a Master Mason.

OFFICERS FROM 1839 TO 1846.

Charles Gear, W. M., 1839–40–1–2–3–4.
H. H. Gear, W. M., 1845.
M. Y. Johnson, W. M., 1846.

SENIOR WARDENS.

E. F. Ogden,   J. Turney,   James Rice,
R. Thomson, W. C. Bostwick.

JUNIOR WARDENS.

T. B. Farnsworth,   J. Turney,   R. Thomson,
John McNulty, Sr.,   A. C. Davis,   H. H. Gear,
M. Faucette, Daniel Wann.

TREASURERS.

Daniel Wann, T. C. Legate, John M. Smith,
John Turney,   John E. Smith, M. P. Silverburgh.

SECRETARIES.

John E. Smith, Walter F. Franklin, Samuel Smoker,
James Rice,   John Turney,   R. Pattison,
M. Y. Johnson, D. H. T. Moss.

MEMBERS NAMES.

Charles Gear,   T. B. Farnsworth, A. T. Crow,

H. H. Gear,   M. Faucette,   S. McLean,
E. W. Turner,   John E. Smith,   John Sherman,
R. Pattison,   James A. Clark,   Geo. M. Mitchell
Daniel Wann,   Samuel Smoker,   C. P. Burrows,
R. Thomson,   W. Warwick,   T. C. Legate.
Thos. Clark,   E. F. Ogden,   D. B. Morehouse
James Craig,   C. Lowe,   R. Dunlap,
D. F. Slitt,   John McNulty, Sr. James Rice,
T. Fanning,   J. S. Crawford,   Daniel Wells,
Philip S. Dade, J. McNulty, Jr.   James N. Hume,
J. N. Johnson,   Wilmot Cady,   John Lane,
James Armour,   J. Parven,   M. Y. Johnson,
             Osee Welch, D. H. Moss,

INITIATED, PASSED AND RAISED.

A. J. Jackson,   John Turney,   J. M. Stanley,
Wm. H. Hooper,   R. M. Long,   A. C. Davis,
Walter F. Franklin Wm. M. Campbell   F. J. Dunn,
Joseph Doplar,   James Stewart,   James Sullivan
Josiah B. Latham,   Samuel Alex,   N. Nadean,
B. W. Whiteside,   L. N. Cummings,   L. Peyton,
N. C. McGrew,   John P. DeZoya,   Nicholas Wall,
— Goble,   P. J. Donevan,   W. C. Bostwick
M. P. Silverburgh, George Houy,   Philip Weber.

In looking over a list of the membership of No.
29, we find those veteran Masonic workers, the Bros.
Gear, one of whom, Capt. H. H. Gear, is at the
present writing a member of all the Masonic bodies
now organized in this city, Lodge, Chapter, Council
and Commandery. Initiated in Massachusetts in the
year 1815, he is now at the advanced age of 82 years,

with a service in the brotherhood of 58 years, still an active, zealous member of the Craft, and bears his Knightly honors with becoming dignity and courtesy, while Charles Gear, the Worshipful Master of Strangers' Union Lodge No. 14 for one or more years, and the Master of Far West Lodge No. 29 for six consecutive years, full of Masonic honors, his life and conduct tried with the unerring square of the Grand Tyler, was admitted to the Grand Lodge above in the year 1861, his funeral being attended by prominent Masons from all the surrounding jurisdictions.

Of the other prominent members of the mother Lodge, Strangers' Union, Bro. James Harris died October 10th, 1829, universally loved and respected by all who knew him, leaving a family honored throughout the North West for their energy and integrity, one son having sought and found Masonic light and Companionship in our present Lodge and Chapter. The same may be said of Bro. Benson Hunt, whose son was long a member of our Lodge. Bros. Moses Meeker, Wm. Hempstead, and all the old members of that " First Lodge " have long since been called upon to give that pass which alone shall gain us admission into those blessed regions of light and life eternal, the Grand Lodge above.

Our researches are amply rewarded in finding the Dispensation granted by M. W. Wm. F. Walker, Grand Master, to the brethren of Far West Lodge. The dispensation bears date June 29th, 1846, and gives our brethren the same name, but changes the number to five, as follows:

"KNO V YE, Therefore, That 1, William F. Walker, Grand Master of the Grand Lodge of the State of Illinois, aforesaid, reposing special trust and confidence in the prudence and fidelity of our Brethren of Far West Lodge above named, have constituted and appointed, and by these presents do constitute and appoint them a regular Lodge of Free and Accepted Masons under our jurisdiction aforesaid, under the name, title and designation allotted to them by our Grand Lodge, to-wit: Far West No 5, hereby ratifying their choice of officers, whereby Brother M. Y. Johnson has been elected Master, Brother Wm C. Bostwick, Senior Warden, and Brother Daniel Wann Junior Warden of this said Lodge "

We have also brought to light the charter bearing date October 8th, 1846, signed by M. W. Nelson D. Morse, G. M., and attested by Levi Lusk, Grand Secretary. This dispensation and charter, carrying with them all the members of No. 29, we shall not repeat their names, but will add those who join by Demit or are Raised in the new Far West Lodge No. 5, which through some caus; to us unknown is chartered as No. 41.

Before pursueing our investigations into the work of Far West under its new Dispensation, we will briefly look for the reason of this change of Charter, and where this " Galena Lodge " mentioned in the closing records of No. 29 came from.

Situated so far from their Grand Lodge as the brethren of No. 29 were, and anxious to send a Representative without so great an expense as required to reach the Grand Lodge of Missouri, they cast about them, first, to sever their connection with Missouri; next, to find the Grand Lodge nearest to them.

Being in the centre of the lead region and having large interests in Wisconsin, the brethren made ap-

plication to that Gran l Lodge, forgetting the well
settled principle of American jurisprudence which
prohibits a Grand Lodge issuing a charter to a subordinate in a State where there is a Grand Lodge established. Tne Grand Lodge of Wisconsin or its G.
M. seemed to have acted in ignorance of the same
law until the prompt action of Grand Master Walker,
of Illinois, and his visit to Galena brought about a
correction of these irregularities.

We have seen that Grand Master Walker did grant
his dispensation to the brethren of No. 29, and the following copy of a paper now before me attests that
they properly severed their connection with the
Grand Lodge of Missouri:

"This is to certify, That Far West Lodge No. 29 has paid up all dues
and arrearages to the Grana Lodge, and agreeable to Resolution of said
Grand Lodge of Missouri, (see proceedings October, 1845, page 26) having
surrendered her charter, has consequently withdrawn from under the
jurisdiction of said Grand Lodge.
"St. Louis, July 7th, 1846.
"FRED. L BILLON, Grand Secretary."

Thinking the consent of the Grand Lodge of Missouri all that was necessary, No. 29 applied for and
received a Dispensation from the Grand Lodge of
Wisconsin, for a Lodge, to be known as " Galena; "
hence, we find this Lodge at work January 2d, 1846,
composed of the same members as No. 29, which did
not cease to exist until June 26th, 1846.

The prompt action of Grand Master Walker in this
matter, brought about the following action of the
Grand Lodge of Wisconsin:

" *Resolved*, That Kavanaugh Lodge and Galena Lodge under Dispensation, be and they are hereby instructed to confer with the Grand Lodge of
Illinois, and ask of that Grand Lodge its sanction to their uniting themselves with this Grand Lodge, and working under its jurisdiction as

other Lodges in this Territory. And that all such correspondence be con-
ducted upon true Masonic principles and fraternal love.
" MADISON, W. T , January 17th, 1846.
Attest:
" Wm. R. SMITH, Grand Secretary."

To this proper request, the members of Galena
Lodge took exceptions, asserting their right to " pe
tition the Grand Lodge of Miss̄ari, Iowa, Illinois, or
Wisconsin." Correct, but only the Grand Lodge of
Illinois could legally grant the request.

The final result was the return of the Dispensation
to the Grand Lodge of Wisconsin, and the acceptance
of one from Illinois.

The records of Galena Lodge U. D. under Grand
Lodge of Wisconsin, record but five meetings and
give the names of the following well known Masons
as officers and members. The first meeting bearing
date January 2d, 1846, and the last March 20th, 1846.

Osee Welch, W. M.　　　　J. Armour, S. W.
Daniel Wann, J. W.　　　　M. P. Silverburgh, Treas.
D. H. T. Moss, Sec.　　　　John E. Smith, S. D.
Wilmot Cady, J. D.　　　　Robt Thomson, Steward.
P. J. Dunnerau, Steward,　Joseph Doplar, Tyler.

And brothers—

M. Y. Johnson,　John P. DeZoya,　II. H. Gear,
A. D. Boyce,　　Geo. M. Mitchell,　Philip Weber,
　　　　　　　A. J. Salame.

Bros. Daniel Wann, John E. Smith and D. H. T.
Moss were appointed a committee to draft suitable
By-Laws, which was done, and the result of their
labors is before us in the form of a printed pamphlet
of eight pages, neatly printed by Messrs H. A. and

H. W. Tenney, of this city. The By-Laws being in the usual form, we make no extracts.

Thus ends Galena Lodge U. D., and we resume our labors in Far West U. D. Nos. 5 and 41, the records of which commence with a copy of the Dispensation from G. M. Walker.

July 17th—Bro. Armour reports having settled all the indebtedness of No. 29, and having a balance of $20. On motion of Bro. Gear it was agreed "to accept the books, stationery and furniture of Galena Lodge U. D., and pay all indebtedness against the same." Communications are held almost every week, and work done in the several degrees.

Oct. 9th—Record shows that Lodge is now held in a building owned by Geo. Roddewig. A good resolution was adopted requiring "all Master Masons coming within the jurisdiction of this Lodge to report themselves as such, otherwise they will be deprived of the benefits and privileges of the same." This is good old Masonry, reaching away back of the old Anderson Constitution of 1721, and if strictly enforced at the present day, would be productive of much good.

While no Mason should neglect his family or business to attend his Lodge, yet all should remember there are duties to be performed by himself, as well as to be required of others. Obligations are not one sided, but mutual. If all were to absent themselves, there would be none to perform those "sacred duties" which constitute the crowning glory of the

Masonic tie: "unsullied honor, unweared industry in the cause of a brother, and universal benevolence." Who that ever knew Bro. Geo. M. Mitchell will fail to picture him as he rises in this meeting and "apologizes to brothers Welch and Johnson?" Who can fail to picture him as with all the manner of a gentleman of the olden time, with all the grace of a courtier, or courtesy of a Red Cross Knight, he asked the brethren to "excuse him for speaking hastily?" Need we say that his excuse was "accepted by the Lodge and the brethren named?" The records say so, so must we. This meeting is full of good things, Just think of the following in the year of our Lord 1874, and yet the youngest of us date back thus far, only 1846!

"Resolved, That all notices from the W. M. addressed to members through the Post Office, be folded and sealed in letter form."

This was before the day of envelopes.

Dec. 28th, 1846, the following officers were elected: John E. Smith, W. M.   James Armour, S. W. Daniel Wann, J. W.   D. H. T. Moss, Treas. W. Cady, Sec.

July 7th, 1847—Lodge of sorrow convened to bury Bro. Joseph Johnson, at which Bro. Chas. Gear, of "Olive Branch Lodge" W. T. presided, many visitors being present.

So far as the records show, the Lodge is doing well, and yet on the 30th day of August a motion is made to surrender the charter, and it was resolved by the "casting vote of the W. M. that a committee be appointed to assist the officers in settling up the affairs of the Lodge."

This, however, was the end of the matter for a season, and the Lodge went along with its work under the same officers until Dec. 27th, St. John's Day, when the following officers were installed:

Geo. W. Woodward, W. M.   A. D. Boyce, S. W.
W. Cady, J. W.   Joseph Harris, Treas.
        John E. Smith, Sec.

The Lodge continued to work until Sept. 1st, 1848, after which time we find no records. What it died of, or how we are unable to tell. The following was its work:

MEMBERS ON DEMIT.

Geo. W. Woodward, Geo. P. Clark, Jas. Ormstead.

RAISED.

Edward Bloomer,   James M. Maughs,   O. D. Boyce,
W. M. Young,   Joseph Harris,   J. B. Coleman,
Alfred S. Gore,   John G. Weiser,   J. Stickle.

From September 1st, 1848, until February 9th, 1854, a period of nearly six years, we have no record that any Masonic body was at work in Galena. At the latter date we find the record of " Phœnix Lodge U. D.," which did some work for one year and a month, and then disappeared as suddenly as it appeared. The only record we can give is as follows:

E. R. Hooper, W. M.   L. J. Germain, S. W.
W. R. Rowley, J. W.   T. M. Wilcox, Treas.
J. E. Smith, Sec.   G. W. Woodward, S. D.
Jacob Davis, J. D.   A. Lovenstein, Tyler.

MEMBERS.

H. H. Gear,   Geo. M. Mitchell,   Geo. G. Gould,
Geo. Houy,   Nathan Meyer.
                 Visitor, Jesse R. Grant.

Dispensation from Grand Lodge òf Illinois read and accepted. ˙

Though the Lodge held a number of meetings and did some work, yet it disappeared before a Charter was granted. Five are the total on whom the third degree was conferred: S. H. Helm, Isaac Shuster, Casper Klett, Max Levi and Hermann Hirschberg.

The visitors to this Lodge were numerous. " Uncle Jesse " being frequently present, as the older members of the present Lodge can attest. A great lover of Masonry, he embraced every opportunity to be present with the Craft.

Masonic darkness is once more upon our city, and no cheerful sound of the gavel is again heard until taken up by that Master Workman, Ely S. Parker, to whose skill as a wise and accomplished Craftsman we are indebted for the present permanent foundation upon which our Masonic bodies so firmly rest, and upon which we trust they will remain until time shall be no more.

Having thus followed the various Lodges which have struggled to maintain themselves, from "Strangers' Union" in 1826, to "Phoenix," in 1855, rejoicing with them in their prosperity, and sympathizing with them in their adversity, we have seen much to admire, amuse, and instruct in these old records. In the hope that our readers have patience enough left to follow us still further, we again take up the record in 1858.

MINERS' LODGE, 273.

A. F. and A. M,

From April 17th, A. L., 5858, to Nov. A. L , 5874.

Jo Daviess Chapter, No. 273, R. A. M.,

From June 9th, A. D. 1859, to Nov. A. D., 1874.

Ely S. Parker Council, No. 60, R. S. E. and S. M.,

July 9th A. D., 1873, to Nov. A. D. 1874.

Galena Commandery No. 40, Knights Templars.

From Sept. 19th, A. D. 1871, to Nov. A. D. 1874.

By-Laws and Masonic history of all the Members of the above named bodies.

MINERS' LODGE, NO. 273.

To the early members of Miners' Lodge we are indebted for the sure foundation upon which they builded our present Masonic edifice, and while it is our earnest desire to award to each his just measure of praise we must concede that to Bro. Ely S. Parker are we principally indebted.

As good citizens and "bright" Masons many of our early members were the equal of Bro. Parker, but, in the qualities which make up the presiding officer, the Worshipful Master, he who is to "rule and govern his Lodge with harmony and regularity;" he who can with tact, grace and dignity, awe into silence—not through fear, but love—by his presence alone. Bro. Parker had no equal. Of commanding presence, and great native dignity, he ruled with a firmness tempered only with fraternal love.

To Bro. P. M., J. C. Spare, we are indebted for the following notice issued to all Master Masons residing in Galena, and which is the oldest Masonic document relating to Miners' Lodge we have been able to find,

MR. J. C. SPARE, ESQ. :

" You are hereby requested to attend a meeting of the Masonic brethren residing in this city and vicinity, on Saturday, Feb. 20th, 1858, at 7½ o'clock, P. M., at the De Soto House."

(Signed)

JOHN E. SMITH.
ROB'T. FRAZER,
EDW'D W. TURNER,
GEO. G. GOULD, Sec.

The subsequent records fail to show that Bro. Spare was present when the Lodge was constituted, or the Corner Stone of the Custom House laid, and yet we know of our own knowledge that he was present on both occasions and assisted in the work.

Our first record bears date as follows :

Miners' Lodge, U. D., Galena, Ill., April 17, 1858.

MEMBERS PRESENT.

Ely S. Parker, W. M.   John E. Smith, S. W. P. T.
M. Y. Johnson, J. W.   M. P. Silverburgh, Treas.
Geo. G. Gould, Sec.   Samuel Frazer, S. D.
          Geo. M. Mitchell, J. D.

VISITORS.

John E. Smith.   Samuel Snider.
W. R. Rowley.   S. H. Helm.
          M. F. Burke.

Those recorded as visitors were resident Masons, who soon became members of the Lodge. The fact that a Lodge so recently constituted did not keep its records more full is an evidence of the difficulty surrounding the "Ancient Records" of the Craft.

In this case many members from Hazel Green, Wisconsin, Elizabeth, and Hanover, in this County, were present, to aid in constituting the Lodge ; and to rekindle the altar fires of Masonry in Galena. A vote of thanks was awarded them and yet not a name appears of record.

So it was of the special communication to lay the Corner Stone of the new Custom House, which was laid with Masonic Honors by Bro. Ely S. Parker, proxy for the M. W. G. M., many brethren from a distance being present and participating, and yet not a record is made of the event other than that at this first meeting : "It was voted to attend the laying of the Corner Stone of the new Custom House, in accordance with Masonic usage," which, as the files of the Galena Advertiser, now Gazette, inform us, was done on this same day, April 17th, 1858.

We cannot follow were we disposed so to do, the workings of Miners' Lodge, No. 273, as closely as we have the Lodges which preceded it. The record is too volumnious, the workmen plenty, and the materi- al at hand to give us full employment in making his- tory, rather than in writing it. The list of member- ship is a volume in itself which speaks more eloquent- ly of the work done, than aught the writer can say. And as for the quality of the material it is before the craft for inspection. We do not hesitate to give our opinion and pronounce it good.

October 15th, 1858.—Miners' Lodge, 273, received its Charter and was duly consecrated. The Officers before mentioned were installed excepting that Bro. E. W. Turner being present assumed his duties as S. W., and Bro, Geo. G. Gould, having removed,Bro. M. F. Burke was made Secretary, Bro. Bond of Mt. Carroll, officiating.

February, 3rd, 1859.—Grand Lecturer Levi Lusk, present, also many visitors from Lena and other Lodges to meet Bro. Lusk

June 24, 1859.—St. John the Baptist's day.—The

brethren of Miners' Lodge, together with their guests
from Hanover, Elizabeth, Shullsburg, Hazel Green,
and Platteville assembled at the Court House, there
formed a procession, preceded by Schreiner's Band,
and marched to their new Hall on Bench Street, formerly known as Mitchell's Hall, which they had fitted
up in a manner suitable to the purposes of the Craft.
.The Hall was dedicated in ample form, Bro. Ely S.
Parker officiating. An address appropriate to the
occasion was delivered by Bro. Parker, a copy of
which was entered in the record book. At the conclusion of the address the large audience composed of
ladies and gentlemen, together with the brethren from
the surrounding country, were dismissed, the visiting
brethren and invited guests being requested to meet
at the De Soto, at 5 P. M., to partake of a banquet.
Among the invited guests were Hon. E. B. Washburne, M. C., Hon. C. B. Denio, and other prominent citizens. After partaking liberally of the lux-
uries of the table, the toasts were announced, and ap-
propriately responded to by Bros. Capt. H. H. Gear,
Ely S. Parker, John S. Williams, of the Press, Dr.
Fowler, of Hanover, Robinson, of Shullsburg, Hons. E.
B. Washburne, C. B. Denio, J. C. Smith and others.

The procession, dedication and festival were each
voted a success, after which Bro. Parker dismissed
the company, each one retiring with the happy thought
" that it were good to have been there."

December 27th, 1859.—St. John the Evangelist's
day.—A grand Masonic and Citizen's dress ball was

given at the De Soto House under the auspices of Miners' Lodge, which was largely attended by the Fraternity and the prominent citizens of Galena. The great feature of the occasion being the entrance of Bro. Ely S. Parker, clothed in the full uniform of a Knight Templar.

The usual routine of Lodge work continued until June 7th, 1861, two funerals having taken place—Bro. Bailey, a Canadian Mason, and the Tyler, Bro. S. H. Helm. At this communication a Lodge of sorrow was held in memory of Bro. U. S. Senator Stephen A. Douglass, who died in the city of Chicago, June 3d, 1861. A committee was appointed to draft resolutions expressive of the great loss sustained by the whole country, north and south, east and west. The nation being on the verge of a deadly struggle for the preservation of the Union, the recent utterances of the great Senator were yet echoing through the land though his voice was hushed in death.

We make the following extract from the report:

"*Resolved,* That the memory of Stephen A. Douglass will be cherished in the precious recollections of his brother Masons, and the bright light of his deeds will assure and encourage posterity to emulate his noble example, as a law giver, as a citizen, and as a Mason."

During the exciting years of the war the Lodge continued to work, though many times it seemed like a hopeless task to get a quorum, so many of the active members being in the military service of the Union. We call to mind of those who were absent, Bros. Gen. Ely S. Parker, afterwards Commissioner of Indian Affairs, Gen. John A. Rawlins, Secretary of War, Gens. John E. Smith, W. R. Rowley, and John C. Smith, Capt. Geo. W. Felt, and others.

To Bro. J. C. Spare, who succeeded Bro. Parker,
in 1861, and Bro. Samuel Snider who for several years
presided over the destinies of Miners' Lodge, together
with the Officers and members who encouraged them
by their regular presence and support, are we indebted for the continuance of work in the Lodge as well
as in Jo Daviess Chapter of Royal Arch Masons.

No event of importance transpired until February,
1866, when the Lodge was called upon to administer
the last sad rites, and give Masonic burial to an old
and active Mason Bro. Geo. M. Mitchell, whose remains had been brought from Memphis, Tenn., to be
buried in the city of his adoption. Upon the records
of Miners' Lodge is found the following tribute to
Bro. Mitchell:

" The members of this Lodge can only cherish, as they do and will, the
memory of a man who was indeed a just and upright Mason."

The regular work of the Lodge continued, and the
Lodge membership increased. Bro. Gen. John A·
Rawlins died in the city of Washington, D. C., Sept.
6th, 1869, which is noted in the records, and the following entry made.

"His work was not done, yet his column is broken. The silver cord is
loosed, the golden bowl is rent in twain ; the dust has returned to the
earth as it was, and the Spirit to God who gave it."

During the year 1872, the question was seriously
agitated of purchasing a lot and building a Masonic
Home. Several pieces of land were examined as were
many buildings, but all falling short of the wants of
the Craft until attention was called to the buildings on
Main, near Warren Street, owned by Messrs. Henry
Corwith and Chas. H. Rogers, which, upon a thor-

ough examination, were found suitable for Masonic purposes, and on July 18th, 1873, the W. M. and Wardens were constituted a Committee, with full power to purchase said buildings " on the best terms to be obtained. "

Plans for alteration of the buildings so as to adapt them to Masonic purposes were then perfected, and at the regular communication Sept. 5th, 1873, the same Committee were directed "to proceed in fitting up the buildings for Masonic purposes, at an expense of not to exceed thirty-five hundred dollars."

It was not, however, until the 25th day of November, 1873, that the buildings were purchased, soon after which the work of demolishing and rebuilding commenced in earnest, and the work was vigorously pushed, under the direction of the Master assisted by Bros. W. R. Rowley, J. B. Young, and S. O. Stillman, until completed and dedicated June 15th, A. D. 1874, A. L. 5874. On this day the several Masonic bodies of the City, assisted by all the Lodges from the surrounding country, joined in a grand procession and proceed to lay the Corner Stone of the new Public Hall of the " Galena Social Turner Society, " with Masonic ceremonies, W. M. J. C. Smith, as proxy of the Grand Master, officiating, assisted by Bros. J. C. Spare, D. G. M., M. Coleman, S. G. W., A. Reynolds, J. G. W., Geo. Broderick, G. Treas., Daniel LeBetter, G. Sec., B. Yerrington, G. S. D., A. J. Louchheim, G. J. D., A. H. Simpson and John Eiseman, Grand Stewards, and J. A. Berryman Grand Tyler.

Having brought our history of Masonry in Galena
from the organization of the first Lodge in 1826, to
the present time, 1874, a period of 49 years, we
most graciously take our leave closing with a report
of the " New Masonic Hall " and the " Dedication, "
as published in the " Galena Gazette. "

DEDICATION OF THE NEW MASONIC TEMPLE—GRAND DOINGS

In accordance with the announcement made through the columns of
the Gazette, the elegant rooms of the Masonic Fraternity of this city
were thrown open for the inspection of the public from 3 o'clock until 6,
of Monday afternoon. The invitations extended to the friends of this
society and the general public, to attend the reception, were gladly accepted, and there was one steady throng of ladies and gentlemen entering during the hours of inspection.

THE COMMITTEE OF ARRANGEMENTS,

consisting of S. K. Miner, R. H. Fiddick, D. LeBetter, C. S. Merrick, J.
R. Davidson, D. N. Corwith, Jesse Crooke, Richard Heller, S. Hunkins.
H. H. Browning, and Daniel Stewart, were indefatigable in their exer-
tions to answer all questions, show all the rooms, main Hall, Prelate
Chamber, Armory, Guard rooms, Tyler's rooms, and Banquet rooms—
even to the place where the famous "goat" is securely housed, and well
fed, all of which being done in a true and courteous manner, pleasing to
the visitor and honorable to the host. In the banquet rooms were found
an unlimited supply of refreshments, not the coarse fare of the Knights
of old, but more in keeping with our modern ideas of what the valiant
Sir Knights deserved and had fairly won.

DEDICATION CEREMONIES.

Seven o'clock found the hall and its various rooms filled with the fair
daughters of Galena, leaving but little space for their gallant attendants.
Among the well known Masons from other places, we recall :
P. M. Capt. H. H. Gear, Iowa ; P. M Dr. A. Campbell, Dunleith ; P.
M's. Hon. J D. Platt, H. H. Peckham, Warren; P. M's. John Weber,
George Marshall, Mark Thomas, Jr., and Henry Glessner. Elizabeth ; P.
M's. Abe Reynolds, Thos. E Moore, and J. G. Love, Hanover ; P. M.
H. Tyrrell, Morseville; P. M. Capt. J. P. Black, Apple River; W. M. Capt.
J. E. Hoover, Shullsburg ; W. M. Jos. Treganza, and P. M. Hon. Geo.
Broderick, Hazel Green.
P. M.'s John C. Spare and M. Y. Johnson, of this city, were also pres-
ent.
W. Bro. H. H. Gear, Master of Ceremonies, announced the following
order of exercises, which were duly executed:

Voluntary on the organ...Selected,
Prof. E. Kempter.
Anthem.................... ...." Awake, Put on thy Strength, "
Galena Musical Union, under leadership of Hon. Bro. R. Seal.
Prayer.................... ....
Bro. Rev. E. H. Downing.
Hymn.... ... ."How beautiful in Zion,"
Galena Musical Union.

CEREMONIES OF DEDICATION.

The Most Worshipful Grand Lodge of Illinois then entered in the following order:

Tyler with drawn sword, Bro. D. Stewart.
Stewards with white rods, Bros. A. H. Simpson and John Eiseman.
Grand Secretary, Bro. D LeBetter.
Grand Treasurer, W. Bro. J. E. Hoover.
Bearer of Great Lights, P. M. A. Reynolds.
Junior Grand Warden, carrying silver vessel with corn, P. M. J. D. Platt,
Senior Grand Warden, carrying a silver vessel with wine, P. M. A Camp-
bell.
Deputy Grand Master, carrying a golden vessel with oil, P. M. John C.
Spare.
The Lodge, carried by four Past Masters, Bros M. Y. Johnson, J. P.
Black, J. G. Love and H H. Peckham.
Book of Constitutions, P. M. Geo. Marshall.
Grand Master, R W. Bro. John C. Smith, supported by Grand Junior
Deacon, Bro. A. J. Louchheim and Grand Senior Deacon
Bro. Jacob Fawcet.

During the entrance of the Grand Lodge, Prof. Kempter presided at
the organ and performed the Grand March, Bro. Senior Warden, M. Coleman, welcomed the Grand Lodge, after which, Bro. S. O. Stillman, on
behalf of his colleagues of the building committee presented the Grand
Master with the keys to the various parts of the building. The Lodge
was then uncovered and the Rev. Bro. E. H. Downing, made an appropriate consecration prayer. The Galena Musical Union then sang the
" Most Excellent Master's Song " as follows :

All hail to the morning
That bids us rejoice ;
The temple's completed,
Exalt high each voice ;
The Cap-stone is finish'd,
Our labor is o'er ;
The sound of the gravel
Shall greet us no more.

To the Power Almighty, who ever has guided
The tribes of old Israel, exalting their fame;
To Him who hath govern'd our hearts undivided,
Let's send forth our voices to praise his great name.

The Grand Junior Warden having presented the Grand Master with
the vessel of corn which he poured upon the Lodge, after which the
grand honors of masonry were given. The singing continued :

Companions assemble
On this joyful day ;
(The Occasion is glorious,)
The key-stone to lay;
Fulfill'd is the promise,
By the Ancient of Days,
To bring forth the cap stone
With shouting and praise.

There is no more occasion for level or plumb line,
For trowel or gavel, for compass or square ;
Our works are completed, the ark safely seated
And we shall be greeted as workmen most rare.

After which, the Grand Senior Warden presented the vessel of wine,

which was pourc l upon the Lodge and the grand honors were twice repeated, closing with the last verse

Almighty Jehovah !
Descend now and fill
This Lodge with thy glory,
Our hearts with good will !
Preside at our meetings,
Assist us to find
True pleasure in teaching
Good will to mankind.
Thy wisdom inspired the great institution
Thy strenth shall support it till nature expire;
And when the creation shall fall into ruin,
Its beauty shall rise through the midst of the fire.

The Deputy Grand Master presents the vessel of oil which is also
poured upon the Lodge, and the grand honors are thrice repeated. The
Grand Chaplain then closed with an invocation, after which, R. W. Bro.
J. C. Smith, delivered the following address :

Ladies, Gentlemen, Brothers, Companions and Illustrious Sir Knights :
—In accordance with a custom which has the sanction of Ancient, Free
and Accepted Masons from the earliest period, we have this evening,ded-
icated this substantial and elegant building to the principles of Free and
Accepted Masons, and to the practice of those Masonic virtues which are
at once the foundation of all that is great and good, and the safeguard of
society, "Virtue, Faith, Hope, and Universal Benevolence," the crowning virtues of our ancient and honorable Order. Justly may the Mason
point with pride to his proud lineage and trace his geneaology from the
dim past, through whose countless ages the grand lessons or Free Masonry have been handed down, and as we have reason to believe will so
continue until time shall be no more. The principles of Free Masonry
are divine and co-eval with that time, when "the earth was without form,
and void." and darkness was upon the face of the deep, and the spirit of
God moved upon the face of the waters, and God said, let there be light
and there was light." Such light as only the angels ever saw, and such
light as every true Mason may hope to see when his earthly pilgrimage
shall be ended, when he shall burst the bonds of mortality, have passed
over the broad river of death; and given the true word and signet, which
shall gain him admission into that Holy of Holies above. Laying aside
the traditions of centuries we may refer to the building of King Solomon's temple as a period in operative Masonry to which we, as speculative Masons, may point with pride, a period when, under the superior
wisdom of our first most excellent Grand Master, Solomon, King of Israel, and his illustrious companions, King Hiram, of Tyre, and the "widow's son," Masonry assumed an organized form. In that great light of
Masonry, (the Holy Bible), now before me, we are informed, that there
were employed in the building of that magnificient temple, three Grand
Masters, 3,600 Masters or Overseers of the work, 80,000 fellow crafts and
70.000 entered apprentices or bearers of burdens. They were so classi-
fied by King Solomon that during the entire period of building the temple, seven and a half years, there was no discord or strife known. When
the temple was completed a day was set apart for its dedication, hence
the custom of dedicating public buildings. The ceremonies of dedication of the magnificent temple erected to the glory of the one ever living
and true God are so well known to all, that I need not dwell upon them.
I may here remark and my attention has been particularly called to the
charge made that we "know not the Savior," I will not enter into a the-

ological discussion upon this point, else I may have to answer many other charges of what we do not know, or what we do not do. It is sufficient to say we are not a religious society founded upon a creed, we are an association of good moral men, and law abiding citizens. Our ceremonies are derived from those which obtained at the building of the first temple. It matters not whether we were constituted at that time, as our traditions teach. It is sufficient that our ceremonies are founded upon that event, and that our symbolic teachings are of the age we represent. We are neither bound nor trammeled by a narrow creed, upon our tesselated floor are found in one harmonious brotherhood, men of every clime and faith. Jewish in our birth, can we exclude the Jew because he believes the Savior has not yet come ! No ! We do not ask the particular creed, but do require that *each* and *every one* who enters the portal of our Lodge have a firm and lasting belief in the existence of the one true and ever living God.

In symbolic Masonry, we have the old dispensation. In Chivalric Masonry in the Commandries of Knights Templars and Knights of Malta, we are governed by the new dispensation. These Orders were founded since the birth, life and death of our Savior, and here, we have the additional requirement of a belief in the death and resurrection of our Lord and Savior   But, I need not dwell upon this subject, our laws and manuals, our professions and our actions are before you, judge what we are, and how worthy we may be of the high esteem in which we are held by all whose good opinion is worth the seeking.

I need not trace our genealogy from the building of the temple of Solomon or Zerubbabel ; our history is to be found in the philosophical societies of ancient Greece and Rome, in the operative Masons of the Middle Ages, and thence down to the speculative Masons of our own day—Masons are not now engaged in the erection of those immense monuments of architecture which seem to defy time and are destined to endure forever, but engaged in the building of a spiritual temple, a house "not made with hands, eternal in the heavens."

The Masons of Galena have a record of which they may well be proud. A Lodge was formed here when this city was but a frontier post. The venerable brother and illustrious Sir Knight, Capt. H. H. Gear, now presiding, who has resided in this city from time immemorial; certainly, so long that "the memory of man runneth not to the contrary," informs me, that he found a lodge at work here in May, 1827, and knows it had been at work for one or two years previous. Records are in my possession of earlier meetings, and in them I find Bro. Gear recorded as a "visitor," at the time he speaks of. This was the "Stranger's Union Lodge," which was afterwards succeeded by "Far West," "Galena" and "Phœnix," from the ashes of which arose our own loved Miners' Lodge, No 273, and its three higher bodies. There are so many pleasant memories clustering about those old Lodges it would be interesting to speak of, but more eloquent than word of mine are the living witnesses who are present with us on this occasion. R. W. Bro. and Illustrious Sir Knight H H. Gear, of Strangers' Union Lodge, who was raised to the sublime degree of a Master Mason, the Thursday preceding the full of the moon in the month of March, 1815, in "Mystic Lodge," Berkshire, Massachusetts, immediately after his discharge from the military service of the United States, having borne a gallant part in the war of 1812.

Bro. and Ill. Sir Knight Daniel Wann, and R. W. Bro. M. Y. Johnson, of Far West, and the succeeding Lodges ; while of our own we have present of those who assisted in its organization:

R. W. Bro. John C. Spare, now officiating as D. G M , and who succeeded to the Chair so long and acceptably filled by the Eminent Bro. whose portrait is to be seen in the west. Bro. Gen. Ely S. Parker, whose absence on this occasion the brethren deeply regret, as they do that of P. M.'s Samuel Snider and T. R. Bird.

Thanking you for the kind interest taken by the citizens, young and old, manifested on this occasion by the large attendance of the fair and brave of this city and surrounding country, I esteem it my pleasure to introduce to you my old friend and companion, R. W. Bro. John C. Spare P. M. of this Lodge.

At the close of the G. M.'s address, P. M. J. C. Spare was introduced, and spoke with much feeling of the early history of Miner's Lodge, and of his pleasant recollections regarding its members, many of whom are absent; Bro. Parker, the first Master, Bro. Snider the third (Bro. Spare being the second), and many others who were detained by business or distance, while not a few had gone to "that bourne from whence no traveler returns."

P. M 's Hon. J. D. Platt, Dr. A. Campbell and Dr J. G. Love, were each introduced, and gave their experience as to the beauties and benefits of Masonry.

The Hon. Judge Wm. Brown, of the Circuit Court, of this District, though not a Mason, was called out, and in sincere and impressive language, told the audience what he knew the Mason- did not do, thereby refuting the slanders of many ignorant persons. The Judge commenced by saying, that it had been a "fixed purpose with him in life, never to speak unless he had something to say, and as this was one of the times when he had nothing to say, he must ask to be excused." We can assure the Judge that if last evening was "one of the times when he had nothing to say," that we, as well as every person present who were fortunate enough to hear him, will deem it a special and lasting favor if he will invite us to be present, when he has something to say.

P. M. Joseph J. P. Black was peculiarly happy in his remarks. His treatment of the aims and purposes of Free Masonry, its friendly and social tie; its grand charities, which, silent and unseen, like the dews of heaven, were carrying blessings to the needy throughout the world, was in exceeding good taste, and unanswerable, while his calm and cutting sarcasm of those who, through "mercenary motives, or willful ignorance," vainly assailed the granite walls of truth presented by Free Masonry, was no doubt prompted by the presence of a known maligner of the craft, one who had not come for the purpose of receiving light, or to reply by argument

Bros. Daniel Wann, a Mason of 45 years, S. O. Stillman and others, were then introduced, adding interest to the occasion.

P. M. H. H. GEAR

moved the audience to tears with his eloquence,calling down the blessings of heaven upon all and as the divine love rested upon all those belonging to the house in which the Ark of the Covenant rested, so this gallant old soldier of 1812, veteran Mason of sixty years and valient Templar prayed for that love to rest upon all entering the portals of Free Masonry. Looking upon the stalwart form of him over whose honored head the summers of eighty-four years have passed, his brethren of the craft were moved to tears. he who had graced the "East" and honored with his presence, every Lodge organized in this city from "Strangers' Union" in 1827, to "Miners" must soon pass "to that rest prepared from the foundation of the world."

DISTINGUISHED VISITORS.

Rev. Bro. Joseph Crummer. Rev. A. C. Smith, Rev. J F. Yates, Hon. James G. Soulard. Hon. F. Stahl, Hon. Bro. H. S. Townsend, Hon. R. H. McClellan, Hon. Thomas J. Sheean, Mayor of the city, John Lorrain. N. Stahl and many others of our prominent and oldest citizens

While of the fair sex who graced the occasion with their presence, space will not permit us to do them justice.

The Galena Gazette, the family newspaper of the Northwest, without which, no Galenian can keep house was spoken of as the source of all news, and as the Editor was present and supposed to know a little of everything, he was loudly called for and introduced. Bro. J. B. Brown made a brief response, and closed by informing the audience that as he was an Editor, he spoke only through the columns of his paper, and would be happy to 'tell them all about it in the Gazette."

"Burn's Farewell" was then rendered by the Galena Musical Union, the brethren all singing.

The Benediction by the Rev. Bro. E. H. Downing, followed after which the audience lingered in seeming regret that the exercises were ended. All feeling that it were good to be there. The Musical Union sang "The Lord is King," with feeling effect.

The audience were then dismissed by W. M., J. C. Smith, who on behalf of the 'Fraters" of Galena, thanked the Brethren of the Lodges of Jo Daviess County, Hazel Green and Shullsburg, large delegations from each of which were present. the ladies and gentlemen of Galena, but particularly Prof. E. Kempter, musical director, Bros. R. Seal, W. Ford and other gentlemen, and especially Mrs. Ford, Miss Bachelor and the ladies of the Galena Musical Union, expressing a hope that all might live long to grace the public receptions and installations of the Masonic Fraternity of Galena.

NEW MASONIC HALL—DESCRIPTION OF THE BUILDING.

The various Masonic bodies of Galena have purchased of Mr. Henry Corwith the two large and substantial brick buildings on Main Street, next north of the Bank of Galena, and have already commenced the work of fitting them up for an elegant Masonic Hall. The deed has been made and the entire amount of purchase money paid down, so that the Fraternity commence the improvements free from debt. The buildings are among the most substantially constructed edifices on Main Street. On the the Main Street front they are four stories high, and five stories on Bench, with an area of 70x36 feet. The two stores on Main Street will be rented for mercantile purposes, together with the room over each, which disposes of the two lower stories.

The third and fourth floors will be converted into one story, and here will be the handsome Masonic Hall which is to comprise an area of 45x30 feet—and 18 feet high. It will be handsomely finished in black and white walnut, with frescoed ceilings, and will be lighted with a double cone reflecting ventilator, with twenty-four gas jets. This is on the Main Street front. The three upper stories of the Bench Street front will be thrown into two stories. On the first floor of these two, will be the Tyler's room, 13x17, and the preparation room, armory and Prelate Chamber, which will be 17x22. These rooms are 11 feet high. Above these are two banquet halls, each 17x22. Alongside the main hall, and running parallel with it, lengthwise, is an area of 50x6 feet, which will be occupied as guard rooms, and Commandery closets for storing the uniforms and equipments of the Knights Templars, the doors having large pannels of French plate glass. All the Masonic apartments will be handsomely frescoed with appropriate Masonic designs,

The work will be in progress during this winter, but as good plastering work cannot be done at this season of the year, the improvements will not be completed till spring It is believed that this will be the finest and most complete Masonic Hall west of Chicago. The plan was conceived, and the purchase of the buildings effected by Gen. J. C. Smith, who is the presiding officer in each of the four Masonic bodies.

CHARTER OF MINERS LODGE, No. 273.

"Sit Lux. Et. Lux, Fuit."

The Most Worshipful Ira A. W. Buck, Esq., Grand Master of the Most Honorable Society of Ancient Free and Accepted Masons, of the State of Illinois :
To all and every—our Right Worshipful Living Brethren—SEND GREET-ING :
KNOW YE, That we, at the petition of our Right Honorable and beloved Brethren Ely S. Parker, E. W. Turner, M. Y. Johnson, Geo. M. Mitchell, Samuel Frazer, Geo. G Gould, and M. P. Silverburgh, and several other Brethren residing in or near Galena, in the County of Jo Daviess and State of Illinois, do hereby constitute the said Brethren into a Regular Lodge of Free and Accepted Masons, to be opened at the aforesaid Galena, by the name of Miners' Lodge, No. 273, and do further, at the said petition and of the great trust, and confidence reposed in the above named Brethren hereby appoint Ely S, Parker, Master, E. W. Turner, Senior Warden, and M. Y- Johnson, Junior Warden. for opening said Lodge, and for such time only as may be thought proper by the Brethren thereof. It being our will that our appointment shall in no wise effect any future election of Officers of that Lodge, but that the same shall be according to the Regulations of the Lodge, and consistent with the general Laws of the Society, contained in the Book of Constitutions.

And we do hereby require you, the said Ely S. Parker, to take special care that all and every, the said Brethren, are or have been *regularly* made *Masons*, and that they do perform and observe and keep all the *Rules* and *Orders* contained in the *Book of Constitutions*, and also such as may from time to time be transmitted to you from us. And further,

That you do from time to time cause to be entered in a book to be kept for that purpose, an account of your proceedings in this Lodge. together with such Regulations as shall be made for the good government thereof, a copy of which, you are in no wise to omit laying before the Grand Lodge once in each year. together with a list of the members of the Lodge. That you annually pay into the Grand Treasury such sums as may be required of you towards the Grand Lodge fund. And moreover, We hereby join and require of you, the said Ely S. Parker, as soon as conveniently may be to send an account in writing of what shall be done by order of these presents.

Given at Springfield, under our hand and seal of Masonry this sixth day of October, A. L. 5858, A. D. 1858.

(SIGNED)   .   IRA A. W. BUCK, G. M.
F, M. BLAIR, D. G. M.
A. J. KUYKENDALL, S. G W.
S. C. Toler, S. G. W.

Attested.   W. G. REYNOLDS,   [SEAL]
Grand Secretary.

BY-LAWS

—OF—

MINERS' LODGE

—OF—

ANCIENT FREE AND ACCEPTED MASONS.

CHARTER GRANTED

OCTOBER 6, 1858.

STATED COMMUNICATIONS

—ON—

FIRST AND THIRD FRIDAYS

OF EACH MONTH,

In Masonic Hall, Galena, Illinois·

BY-LAWS.

ARTICLE I.

NAME.

SEC. 1. This Lodge shall be known by the name of MINERS' LODGE, No. 273, Ancient Free and Accepted Masons.

ARTICLE II.

OF WHOM CONSISTING.

SEC. 1. This Lodge shall consist of a Worshipful Master, Senior Warden, Junior Warden, Treasurer, Secretary, Senior Deacon, and Junior Deacon, Chaplain, two Stewards, a Tyler, and such brethren as may be constitutionally admitted members.

ARTICLE III.

OF OFFICERS.

SEC. 1. The Worshipful Master, Wardens, Treasurer and Secretary, shall be elected at the regular communication, next before the festival of St. John, the Evangelist, in each year, (Dec. 27,) and shall be installed at the same or some special communication, on or before Saint John's day, Dec. 27, of each year, and shall hold their offices until their successors shall be duly installed.

Sec. 2. In all elections a majority of the whole

number of votes given shall be necessary to a choice.

SEC. 3. The Senior Deacon, Chaplain and Tyler shall be appointed by the Worshipful Master, the Junior Deacon by the Senior Warden, and the Stewards by the Junior Warden. All other officers and all committees shall be appointed by the Worshipful Master.

ARTICLE IV.

DUTIES OF OFFICERS.

SEC. 1. The Worshipful Master shall preside at all meetings of the Lodge; shall have charge of the Dispensation or Charter, which he shall have present in the Lodge when open; shall see that the Ancient Constitutions and Landmarks, and that the Constitution, laws and regulations of the Grand Lodge are obeyed, and that the officers and members faithfully perform their Masonic duties.

SEC. 2. The Worshipful Master shall have the right to call special communications; to open, close, or call off the Lodge at pleasure,—but shall not permit appeals to be taken from his decisions on any questions, he being ameanable for his conduct in the government of the Lodge to the Grand Lodge or Grand Master only.

SEC. 3. All other duties of the Master shall be such as are required by Masonic usage, and our time-honored Masonic Ritual.

SEC. 4. The Wardens shall assist the Worshipful Master in conducting the business of the Lodge. In the absence or disability of the Master, the Senior

Warden shall preside, and shall, for the time being, be entitled to all his privileges, and shall be vested with all his powers. In the absence or disability of the Master and Senior Warden, the Junior Warden shall succeed to the same rights, powers and privileges, and in the absence of the Master and both Wardens the Lodge cannot be opened for any purpose, except by the Grand Master or his Special Deputy.

SEC. 5. The Treasurer shall receive all moneys from the hands of the Secretary, and give his receipt therefor. He shall pay all orders and bills drawn on him by the Worshipful Master, with the consent of the Lodge, when attested by the Secretary. He shall keep an exact record of all his acts appertaining to his office, in a suitable book procured for that purpose, and shall at all times hold his accounts, vouchers and funds, subject to the inspection of the Master, Lodge, or its authorized committee; and shall be fore entering upon the duties of his office, give a bond with good security, for the faithful performance of the duties of his office, to be approved by the first three officers of the Lodge.

SEC. 6. The Secretary shall keep a true and correct record of all the proceedings of the Lodge proper to be written, and preserve in appropriate files all papers and documents relating thereto; issue all notices when required; make the necessary returns to the Grand Lodge; receive all moneys paid into the Lodge, and pay the same over to the Treasurer, taking his receipt therefor. He shall be exempt from

dues, and receive in addition thereto, $1.00 for each
meeting of the Lodge, 25 cents for each Demit, and
$1.00 for each Diploma, to be paid by the applicant,
together with such other compensation for extra services as the Lodge may from time to time determine.

SEC. 7. The Tyler shall tyle the Lodge faithfully, go on errands, attend the sittings of committees, if
required, serve summons, and keep the Lodge and
ante-rooms, with all their furniture, neat and in good
order. He shall receive $1.00 for each communica-
tion of the Lodge, or meeting of its committees, and
be exempt from all dues.

SEC. 8. The Master and Wardens shall constitute
a standing committee, whose duty it shall be to examine and adjust all accounts presented to the Lodge, to
compare and audit the Treasurer and Secretary's account, when necessary, and report on the same. It
shall be their duty to hear and settle private difficulties between members; and in case of the sickness of
a brother, they shall see that said brother is furnish-
ed with suitable comforts, together with medical aid
—watchers if necessary; also, to afford assistance to
the needy and distressed Mason, his widow and or-
phans, when they may think it necessary and pru-
dent. They may draw on the Treasurer for any sum
not exceeding $10.00 at any one time, and shall re-
port all their proceedings to the Lodge.

SEC. 9. No brother shall be elected Master who
has not been duly elected, installed, and served as
Warden, except in case of emergency, and then by

authority—by dispensation from the Grand Master·

ARTICLE V.

VACANCIES.

SEC. 1. In case of the death, removal, suspension or expulsion of either of the Wardens, Treasurer, Secretary, or Senior Deacon, the vacancy shall be supplied by appointment of the Master. A vacancy in the office of Junior Deacon shall be supplied by the Senior Warden.

A vacancy in the office of Steward shall be supplied by the Junior Warden. All other vacancies shall be supplied by the Master.

SEC. 2. No officer shall resign or Demit after he has been duly installed.

ARTICLE VI.

OF MEMBERSHIP.

SEC. 1. Master Masons, after producing a proper Demit may be admitted to membership in this Lodge, upon petition, regularly recommended in writing, at a regular meeting, after a favorable report of a committee of inquiry, at the regular communication thereafter, and a unanimous ballot of the members present, and on paying the sum of $5.00.

SEC. 2. Candidates applying for admission shall be men " under the tongue of good report; " of good moral character, and believers in God; twenty-one years of age; upright in body, with the senses and organs of men, and not deformed or dismembered; in the full possession of their moral and intellectual faculties; in the unrestrained enjoyment of civil and personal liberty, and this, too, by the birthright of inheritance, and not in consequence of release of themselves or immediate progenitors from hereditary bondage.

Sec. 3. Every petition for initiation in this Lodge shall be in writing, and shall be presented and read at a regular communication ; shall be accompanied with a fee of $5.00, and shall be referred to a committee of three members, who shall carefully examine into the character and standing of the petitioner, and make report thereof at the second regular communication hereafter.

Sec. 4. Upon the report of the committee, whether favorable or unfavorable, the Lodge shall, at the same or some subsequent regular communication, proceed to ballot.

Sec. 5. No ballot for any purpose shall be taken at any but a regular communication, unless by authority of a Dispensation from the Grand Master.

Sec. 6. In balloting for candidates for initiation or for membership, all members of the Lodge present shall vote,—for according to an old regulation, " no man can be entered a brother in any particular Lodge, or admitted to be a member thereof, without the unanimous consent of all the members of that Lodge then present when the candidate is proposed;" nor shall a member be excused from the performance of this important duty, except by the unanimous consent of all the members present. No Mason shall be required by the Master or Lodge to give his reasons for the vote which he has deposited.

SEC. 7. After the ballot has been taken and duly examined, first, by the Wardens and finally by the Master, the result shall be declared by the Master. In case of a negative vote, the Master may order a second, and even a third passing of the ballot, to avoid the possibility of a mistake; but when declared as aforesaid, shall in all cases be final and cannot be set aside.

SEC. 8. It shall not be in order to move the reconsideration of a ballot which has been declared on the petition of a candidate for initiation or membership, neither shall the Master entertain any such motion at any time.

SEC. 9. No candidate shall receive more than one degree on the same day, nor shall a higher degree be conferred on any brother at a less interval than four weeks from his receiving a previous degree without special Dispensation from the Grand Master; nor unless he has passed a satisfactory examination in open Lodge on the degree or degrees taken.

SEC. 10. All Masons, raised to the sublime degree of Master Mason, and all Master Masons admitted as members, after signing the By-Laws, shall be entitled to all the rights of membership in this Lodge.

ARTICLE VII.
FEES AND DUES.

SEC. 1. The fees for the Degrees conferred in this Lodge shall be as follows:

For that of Entered Apprentice,   -   - $15.00
For that of Fellow Craft, -   -   -   - 10.00
For that of Master Mason,   -   -   -   10.00
And in no case shall the three degrees be conferred for a less sum than $35.00, and the fees shall in all cases be received before the candidate shall be initiated. A Fellow Craft having received the second degree in any other Lodge, shall pay $5.00 in addition to the regular fee for raising, and the same shall accompany his petition.

SEC. 2. In all cases where an application for initiation is rejected, the money shall be returned, with information of the rejection; which information shall in no case be communicated by any member of this Lodge, or any visitor who may be present, to one not a Mason, under the penalty, in the former case, of exclusion from the Lodge; in the latter, of never again being admitted to visit. The same shall apply to the disclosure of any of the proceedings of the Lodge. The Worshipful Master shall frequently cause this section to be read in open Lodge.

Sec. 3. Every member shall pay $3.00 per annum in advance as Lodge dues, and if not paid within the year, such member shall not be entitled to vote at the annual election, and shall be ineligible to office.

The year shall commence on the first day of January. Each member who is one year in arrears for dues, and still neglects to pay, after due notice from the Secretary, may be indefinitely suspended, unless from indigence, or other good reason, by a unanimous vote of the Lodge he shall be exempted from payment.

ARTICL VIII.

DEMITS.

SEC. 1. Master Masons, members in good standing, free from charges and not in arrears for dues,shall be entitled to Demits for one only of the following reasons, (upon the payment of fees :)

First, In case of residence without the jurisdiction of the Grand Lodge of Illinois.

Second, In case of a desire to join another Lodge in the same city or town, or a Lodge nearer to the residence of the applicant than this Lodge.

Third, In case of a desire to assist in the formation of a new Lodge.

SEC. 2. Members of the Lodge in good standing shall be entitled to a Lodge diploma on paying to the Secretary the cost of the same, and the fee of one dollar.

All applications for Demits shall be made in writing, signed by the applicant, be presented to the Lodge at a stated communication. Shall be read in open lodge, and lie over until the next or some subsequent stated meeting, when if the applicant's dues are paid, and there are no charges against him, a Demit may be granted by a vote of the majority of the members present.

ARTICLE IX.

MEETINGS.

SEC. 1. The regular communications of this Lodge shall be held on the First and Third Fridays of each month. The hours for working shall be from 7½ o'clock until 10 o'clock in the evening.

SEC. 2. The Lodge shall in all cases proceed to open within fifteen minutes after the stated time for assembling if a sufficient number of Masons be present.

ARTICLE X.

DISCIPLINE AND JURISDICTION.

SEC. 1. This Lodge has full power and authority to exercise penal jurisdiction over all Masons, unaffiliated, or affiliated, as well as members of this Lodge, within its jurisdiction, for violation of moral and Masonic law.

SEC. 2. All Masons are bound by their tenure to obey both the moral and Masonic law, for every Mason should live honestly, injure nobody, and render to every one their just due; should conform to the rules specified in the Ancient Charges, and follow the moral and Masonic precepts laid down in our time-honored ritual forms and ceremonies; hence, profanity, impiety, neglect of social and domestic duties, murder, cruelty, adultery, dishonesty, perjury, malevolence, falsehood, coveteousness, gambling, drunkenness, and the numerous other vices injuriously affecting the relations of man to God, his neighbor and himself; unseemingly or irreverent conduct in the Lodge; private piques and quarrels, brought into the Lodge; imprudent conversation in relation to Masonry in the presence of uninitiated strangers; withholding relief when applied for by a worthy brother, wrangling, quarreling, backbiting and slander; improper revelations; undue solicitations for candidates; angry and over-zealous arguments in favor of Masonry with its enemies; all acts tending to impair the unsullied purity of the order; want of reverence for, and obedience to Masonic superiors; expressing contemptuous opinions of the original rulers and patrons of Masonry, or of the institution itself; countenancing imposters; holding Masonic intercourse with clandestine Masons; or visiting irregular lodges;—are, all and each, violations of moral and Masonic law, and are, therefore, Masonic crimes, for which the perpetrators shall be amenable to Masonic punishment.

Sec. 3. The Masonic punishment which may and shall be inflicted by this Lodge for the moral and Masonic crimes thus specified, shall be in either one of the following grades, to-wit:

1st. Reprimand.

2d. Definite Suspension.

3d. Indefinite suspension,

4th. Expulsion from the Lodge, and consequently expulsion from all the rights and privileges of Masonry.

Sec. 4. All trials in this Lodge shall be as follows:

1. A regular charge, in writing, specifying the nature of the offense, and signed by the accuser, shall be delivered to the Secretary, who shall read it at the next regular communication, at which time the Worshipful Master shall appoint the time for trial, of which it shall be the duty of the Secretary to give due and timely notice to the accused, who shall be en-

titled to a copy of the charges, and to ample time and opportunity to prepare his defense.

2. All trials shall be in the Lodge of the highest degree to which the accused has attained, in which the examination of witnesses shall take place in the presence of both the accused and accuser, who shall have the right to be present at all examinations of witnesses, in or out of the Lodge, and to propose such relevent questions as they may desire.

3. After the trial is concluded the accused and the accuser shall be requested to retire, and in case the trial has been in a Lodge of Entered Apprentices or Fellow Crafts, the Lodge shall then be opened on the third degree, for no decision shall be made for or against a brother, after regular trial, except in a Master Mason's Lodge, in which the question of "Guilty" or "Not Guilty," shall be put by the Master, in which all the members present shall be required to vote, and of which two-thirds shall be in the affirmative, or the accused shall be declared "Not Guilty."

4. If the verdict is "Guilty" the Master or presiding Officer shall put the question as to the amount of punishment, beginning with the highest and ending with the lowest Masonic punishment herein provided. The vote on the nature of the punishment may be taken by a show of hands, and decided by a two-thirds vote of the members present.

5. Should the accused member believe that the proceedings had against him have been informal or irregular, whereby he has suffered, he can carry the

matter up before the Grand Lodge, by appeal, by leaving a notice of appeal with the Secretary of the Lodge, and also with the Grand Secretary, one month before the next annual communication of the Grand Lodge.

6. If the residence of the accused is not known, or, if upon due summons, he refuses or neglects to attend, this Lodge may proceed to trial without his presence.

7. The testimony of Masons shall be taken in Lodge or in Committee; that of competent persons, not Masons, by a Committee on oath, administered by a competent legal officer, and may be by affidavit.

8. A member cannot be suspended for non-payment of dues without written notice and a fair trial.

9. The witnesses in all Masonic trials, whether Masons or not, shall be persons who have their reason, and such religious belief as to feel the obligations of an oath; who have not been convicted of any infamous crime, and who are not influenced by interest or malevolence.

ARTICLE XI.
DUTIES OF BRETHREN.

It is particularly enjoined by this Lodge that all its members treat each other with kindness and decorum, avoiding all slander, malice and unjust resentment, and talking disrespectfully of a brother's person or performance, by which the character of a brother may be injured, his feelings wounded, or the most excellent tenets of our Order, [Friendship, Moralty and Brotherly Love,] be violated or in any degree intercepted in their exercise; nor must they suffer any to spread unjust reproaches or calumnies against a brother be hind his back, nor to injure him in his fortune, reputation or character; but they shall defend such brother, and give him notice of any danger or injury wherewith he may be threatened, to enable him to escape the same, as far as is consistent with honor, prudence, and the safety of Religion, Morality and the State, but no further. Hypocrisy and deceit should be unknown among Masons; sincerity and plain dealing should distinguish them, and heart and tongue join in promoting each other's welfare.

ARTICLE XII.

AMENDMENTS.

No part of these By-Laws shall be repealed, altered, annulled, suspended or amended, unless a proposition in writing shall have been presented at a stated meeting, at least four weeks previous to its consideration, when, if two-thirds of the members present vote in favor of the proposal it shall be adopted.

ARTICLE XIII.

RULES OF ORDER.

RULE 1. When the W. M. takes the chair, the brethren shall retire to their respective places, and shall observe profound silence.

RULE 2. ORDER OF BUSINESS:

1. Reading of the Minutes.
2. Reading and referring of Petitions.
3. Reports of Committees.
4. Balloting.

5. Work.

6. Unfinished Business.

6. New Business.

RULE 3. No brother will be permitted to leave his seat, or move from one part of the room to another, except such as may be required to do so in the performance of their duty, without permission from the Worshipful Master.

RULE 4. Every brother shall stand up when he speaks, and shall address the Worshipful Master in a respectful and Masonic manner; he shall speak but once upon any subject, unless it be merely to explain, until every member present who chooses to avail him-self of the privilege has spoken.

RULE 5. On all motions and debates, parliamentary rules shall be adhered to, as far as the regulatious of the Grand Lodge of Illinois and the ancient usages of Masonry will permit.

RULE 6. The Worshipful Master shall rule and govern with order and regularity all the communications of the Lodge.

RULE 7. When a question is put every member shall vote thereon, unless for special reasons he shall be excused by the Lodge, according to the By-Laws.

RULE. 8. In order to preserve on all occasions the dignity of the Oriental Chair, all debates shall cease and strict silence be observed when the Worshipful Master rises.

RULE 9. The Worshipful Master shall cause the

Constitution, Laws and Regulations of the Grand Lodge, together with these By-Laws, to be frequently read in this Lodge, that none may pretend ignorance of the excellent precepts they enjoin.

THE OLD CHARGES

OF THE

FREE AND ACCEPTED MASONS,

OLLECTED FROM THEIR RECORDS.

AS PUBLISHED BY THE

GRAND LODGE OF ENGLAND,

1722.

AND THE

GRAND LODGE OF ILLINOIS,

1854.

I   CONCERNING GOD AND RELIGION.

A Mason is obliged by his tenure to obey the moral law ; and if he rightly understands the Art he will never be a stupid atheist, nor an irreligious libertine. But though in ancient times Masons were charged in every country to be of the religion of that country or nation, whatever it was; yet it is now thought

more expedient only to oblige them to that religion
in which all men agree, leaving their particular
opinions to themselves; that is, to be *good men and
true*, or men of honor and honesty, by whatever de-
nominations or persuasions they may be distinguished, whereby Masonry becomes the *centre of
union*, and the means of conciliating true friendship
among persons that must have remained at a perpetual distance.

II OF THE CIVIL MAGISTRATE, SUPREME AND SUBORDINATE.

A Mason is a peaceable subject to the civil powers
wherever he resides or works, and is never to be concerned in plots and conspiracies against the peace and
welfare of the nation, nor to behave himself unduti-
fully to inferior Magistrates; for as Masonry hath been
always injured by war, bloodsheed and confusion, so
ancient Kings and Princes have been much disposed
to encourage the Craftsmen, because of their peace-
ableness and *loyalty*, whereby they particularly an-
swered the cavils of their adversaries, and promoted
the honor of the fraternity, who ever flourished in
times of peace. So that if a Brother should be a
rebel against the State, he is not to be countenanced
in his rebellion, however he may be pitied as an un-
happy man, and if convicted of no other crime,
though the loyal brotherhood must and ought to dis-
own his rebellion, and give no umbrage or ground of

political jealousy to the government for the time being, they cannot expel him from the Lodge, and his
relation to it remains indefeasible.

III OF LODGES

A Lodge is a place where Masons assemble and
work; hence that assembly, or duly organized society
of Masons, is called a Lodge; and every Brother
ought to belong to one, and be subject to its *By-Laws*,
and general regulations. It is either *particular* or
general, and will be best understood by attending it,
and by the regulations of the General or Grand Lodge
hereunto annexed. In ancient times, no Master or
Fellow could be absent from it, especially when
warned to appear at it, without incurring a severe
censure, until it appeared to the *Master* and *Wardens*
that necessity hindered him.

The persons admitted members of a Lodge, must
be good and true men—free born, and of mature and
discreet age. No bond-men, no women, no immoral
or scandalous men, but of good report

IV. OF MASTERS, WARDENS, FELLOWS AND APPRENTICES.

All preferment among Masons is grounded upon
real worth, and personal merit only; that so the Lords
may be well served—the Brethren not put to shame,
nor the Royal Craft despised ; therefore, no Master
or Warden is chosen by seniority, but for his merit.

It is impossible to describe these things in writing, and every brother must attend in his place, and learn them in a way peculiar to this fraternity. Only candidates may know that no Master should take an Apprentice, unless he have sufficient employment for him, and unless he be a perfect youth, having no maim or defect in his body, that may render him incapable of learning the Art—of serving his Master's Lord, and of being made a Brother and then a Fellow Craft in due time, even after he has served such a term of years as the custom of the country directs; and that he should be descended of honest parents that so, when otherwise qualified, he may arrive to the honor of being the Warden, and then the Master of the Lodge, the Grand Warden, and at length the Grand Master of all the Lodges, according to his merit.

No Brother can be a Warden until he has passed the part of a Fellow Craft; nor a Master until he has acted as a Warden; nor Grand Warden until he has been Master of a Lodge; nor Grand Master unless he has been a Fellow Craft before his election, who is also to be nobly born, or a gentleman of the best fashion, or some eminent scholar, or some curious architect, or other artist, descended of honest parents and who is of singular great merit in the opinion of the Lodges. And for the better and easier and more honorable discharge of his office, the Grand Master has a power to choose his own Deputy Grand Master who must be then, or must have been formerly, the

Master of a particular Lodge, and has the privilege of acting whatever the Grand Master, his principal should act, unless the said principal be present, or interpose his authority by a letter.

These rulers and governors, supreme and subordinate, of the ancient Lodge, are to be obeyed in their respective stations by all the brethren, according to the old. charges and regulations, with all humility, reverence, love and alacrity.

V OF THE MANAGEMENT OF THE CRAFT IN WORKING.

All Masons shall work honestly on working days' that they may live creditably on holy days, and the time appointed by the law of the land or confirmed by custom, shall be observed.

The most expert of the Fellow Craftsmen shall be chosen or appointed the Master or Overseer of the Lord's work, who is to be called Master by those that work under him. The Craftsmen are to avoid all ill language, and to call each other by no disobliging name but Brother. or Fellow, and to behave themselves courteously within and without the Lodge.

The Master, knowing himself to be able of cunning shall undertake the Lord's work as reasonably as possible, and truly dispend his goods as if they were his own; nor to give more wages to any Brother or Apprentice, than he really may deserve.

Both the Master and the Masons receiving their wages justly, shall be faithful to the Lord, and honestly finish their work, whether *task* or *journey;* nor put the work to *task* that hath been accustomed to *journey.*

None shall discover envy at the prosperity of a Brother, or supplant him, or put him out of his work, if he is capable to finish the same; for no man can finish another's work so much to the Lord's profit, unless he be thoroughly acquainted with the designs and draughts of him that began it. When a Fellow Craftsman is chosen Warden of the work, under the Master, he shall be true both to Master and Fellows, shall carefully oversee the work in the Masters absence, to the Lords profit, and his brethren shall obey him.

All Masons employed, shall receive their wages, without murmuring or mutiny, and not desert the master till the work is finished.

A younger Brother shall be instructed in working to prevent spoiling the materials for want of judgment, and for increasing and continuing of brotherly love.

All the tools used in working shall be approved by the Grand Lodge.

No laborer shall be employed in the proper work of Masonry: nor shall Free Masons work with those that are not free, without an urgent necessity; nor shall they teach laborers and *unaccepted* Masons as they should teach a Brother or Fellow.

VI. OF BEHAVIOR, VIZ.

1. In the Lodge, while constituted, you are not to
hold private Committees, or separate conversation,
without leave from the Master, nor to talk of anything impertinent or unseemly, nor interrupt the Master or Wardens, or any Brother speaking to the Master; nor behave yourself ludicrously or jestingly
while the Lodge is engaged in what is serious and
solemn, nor use any unbecoming language upon any
pretence whatsoever, but to pay due reverence to your
Master, Wardens, and Fellows, and put them to wor-
ship.

If any complaint be brought, the Brother found
guilty, shall stand to the award and determination of
the Lodge, who are the proper and competent judges
of all such controversies, (unless you carry it by appeal to the Grand Lodge,) and to whom they ought
to be referred, unless a Lord's work be hindered the
meanwhile, in which case a particular reference may
be made ; but you must never go to law about what
concerneth Masonry, without an absolute necessity
apparent to the Lodge.

2 *Behavior after the Lodge is over, and the brethren not gone.*—You may enjoy yourselves with inno-
cent mirth, treating one another according to ability;
but avoiding all excess, or forcing any Brother to eat
or drink beyond his inclination, or hindering him
from going when his occasions call him, or doing or

saying anything offensive, or that may forbid an easy and free conversation, for that would blast our harmony and defeat our laudable purposes. Therefore, no private piques or quarrels must be brought within the door of the Lodge, far less any quarrels about religion or nations, or State policy. We being only, as Masons, of the Catholic religion above mentioned; we are also, of all nations, tongues, kindreds, and languages, and are resolved against all politics, as what never yet conduced to the welfare of the Lodge, nor ever will. This charge has been always strictly enjoined and observed; but especially, since the reformation in Britain, or the dissent and secession of these nations from the communion of Rome.

3. *Behavior when brethren meet without strangers, but not in a Lodge formed*—You are to salute one another in a courteous manner, as you will be instructed—calling each other Brother; freely giving mutual instruction, as shall be thought expedient, without being overseen or overheard, and without encroaching upon each other, or derogating from that respect which is due to any Brother were he not a Mason; for though all Masons are as brethren upon the same *level*, yet Masonry takes no honor from a man that he had before; nay, rather it adds to his honor, especially if he has deserved well of the Brotherhood, who must give honor to whom it is due, and avoid ill manners.

4. *Behavior in presence of strangers* NOT Masons.—You shall be cautious in your words and car

riage, that the most penetrating stranger shall not be
, able to discover or find out what is not proper to be
intimated; and sometimes you shall divert a discourse,
and manage it prudently, for the honor of the worshipful fraternity.

5. *Behavior at home, and in your neighborhood.*
—You are to act as becomes a moral and wise man;
particularly, not to let your family, friends, and neigh-
bors, know the concerns of the Lodge, &c., but
wisely to consult your own honor, and that of the ancient brotherhood, for reasons not to be mentioned
here. You must also consult your health, by not
continuing together too late, or too long from home
after Lodge hours are past, and by avoiding of glut-
tony and drunkenness, that your family be not neg-
lected or injured, nor you disabled from working.

6 *Behavior towards a strange Brother.*—You are
cautiously to examine him in such a method as prudence shall direct you, that you may not be imposed
upon by an ignorant, false pretender, whom you are
to reject with contempt and derision, and beware of
giving him any hints of knowledge; but if you discover him to be a true and genuine Brother, you are
to respect him accordingly; and if he is in want you
must relieve him if you can, or else direct him how
he may be relieved; you must employ him some days,
or else recommend him to be employed. But you
are not charged to do beyond your ability—only to
prefer a poor Brother, that is a *good man and true*

before any other poor people in the same circum-
stance.

Finally, all these charges you are to observe, and
also those that shall be communicated to you in *another way*—cultivating brotherly love, the foundation
and cap-stone—the cement and glory of this ancient
fraternity, avoiding all wrangling and quarreling—all
slander and backbiting, not permitting others to slander any honest Brother, but defending his character,
and doing him all good offices, as far as is consistent
with your honor and safety, and no farther; and if
any of them do you injury, you must apply to your
own or his Lodge, and from thence you may appear
to the Grand Lodge at the Quarterly Communication,
and from thence to the annual Grand Lodge, as has
been the ancient laudable conduct of our forefathers
in every nation—never taking a legal course but when
the case cannot be otherwise decided, and patiently
listening to the honest and friendly advice of Master
and Fellows, when they would prevent your going
to law with strangers, or would excite you to put
a speedy period to all law-suits, that so you may
mind the affairs of Masonry with more alacrity and
success. But with respect to Brothers or Fellows
at law, the Master and Brethren should kindly offer
their mediation, which ought to be thankfully submitted to by the contending Brethren, and if that
submission is impracticable, they must, however,
carry on their process, or law-suit, without wrath

and rancour, (not in the common way,) saying or
doing nothing which may hinder brotherly love,
and good offices to be renewed and continued, that
all may see the *benign* influence of Masonry, as all
true Masons have done from the beginning of the
world, and will do to the end of time. AMEN.
SO MOTE IT BE.

OFFICERS AND MEMBERS.

OFFICRES—1862.

Samuel Snider, W. M. S. O. Stillman, S. W.
Geo. M. Mitchell, J. W. M. P. Silverburgh, Treas.
J. C. Smith, Sec. A. L. Rogers, S. D.
J. M. Spratt, J. D. M. Faucette, Tyler.

OFFICERS.—1863.

Samuel Snider, W. M. T. Hallet, S. W.
T. R. Scott, J. W. M. P. Silverburgh, Treas.
S. O. Stillman, Sec. A. L. Rogers, S. D.
J. M. Spratt, J. D. O. Marble, Tyler.

OFFICERS.— 1864.

Samuel Snider, W. M. T. R. Bird, S. W.
Daniel Stewart, S. W. M. P. Silverburgh, Treas.
S. O. Stillman, Sec. A. L. Rogers, S. D.
J. M. Spratt, J. D. M. Faucette, Tyler.

OFFICERS.—1865.

Samuel Snider, W. M. Geo. M. Mitchell, S. W.
A. L. Rogers, J. W. M. P Silverburgh, Treas.
S. O. Stillman, Sec. Samuel Frazer, S. D.
J. M. Spratt, J. D. M. Faucette, Tyler.

OFFICERS.—1866.

Samuel Snider, W. M. A. L. Rogers, S. W.
Geo. L. Shears, J. W. M. P Silverburgh, Treas.
S. O. Stillman, Sec. T. R. Bird, S. D.
M. M. Miller, J. D. J. B. Young, Tyler.

OFFICERS.—1867.

Samuel Snider, W. M. T. R. Bird, S. W.
Samuel Frazer, J. W. J. M. Spratt, Treas.

S. O. Stillman, Sec.　　　M. M. Miller, S. D.

J. C. Spare, J. D.　　　Chas. Semmern, Tyler.

OFFICERS.—1868.

T. R. Bird, W. M.　　　Daniel Stewart, S. W.

B. J. Ewing, J. W.　　　J. M. Spratt, Treas.

S. O. Stillman, Sec.　　　Daniel LeBetter, S. D.

S. K. Miner, J. D.　　　C. Koontz, Tyler.

OFFICERS.—1869.

A. Campbell, W. M.　　　J. C. Spare, S. W.

S. K. Miner, J. W.　　　J. M. Spratt, Treas.

S. O. Stillman, Sec.　　　Daniel LeBetter, S. D.

C. F. Miller, J. D.　　　F. S. Koontz, Tyler.

OFFICERS.—1870.

J. C. Smith, W. M.　　　D. LeBetter, S. W.

Wm. Passmore, J. W.　　　J. M. Spratt, Treas.

S. O. Stillman, Sec.　　　John W. Luke, S. D.

Edward Jones, J. D.　　　F. S. Koontz, Tyler.

OFFICERS.—1871.

J. C. Smith, W. M.　　　Wm. Passmore, S. W.

S. K. Miner, J. W.　　　J. M. Spratt, Treas.

S. O. Stillman, Sec.　　　Rev. E. H. Downing, Chap.

D. LeBetter, S. D.　　　A. J. Louchheim, J. D.

D. Stewart, Tyler.

OFFICERS.—1872.

J. C. Smith, W. M.　　　S. K. Miner, S. W.

D. LeBetter, J. W.　　　J. M. Spratt, Treas.

S. O. Stillman, Sec.　　　Rv. E. H. Downing, Chp

H. H. Oldenhage, S. D.　　　R. H. Fiddick, J. D.

D. Stewart, Tyler.

OFFICERS.—1873.

J. C. Smith, W. M.	H. H. Oldenhage, S. W
J. W. Wann, J. W.	J. M. Spratt, Treas.
Daniel LeBetter, Sec.	Rv. E. H. Downing,Ch
L. A. Rowley, S. D.	C. S. Merrick, J. D.

D. Stewart, Tyler.

OFFICERS.—1874.

J. C. Smith, W. M.	M. Cóleman, S. W.
C. S. Merrick, J. W.	J. M. Spratt, Treas.
Daniel LeBetter, Sec.	Rv. E. H. Downing,Chp
T. E. Armitstead, S. D.	A. J. Louchheim, J. D

D. Stewart, Tyler.

MEMBERS ADMITTED ON DEMIT OI RAISED.

---

§ Demitted. ‡ Honorary. † Deceased. ‖ Suspended
* Expelled.

Ely S. Parker,	‡ April 17th, 1858.
E. W. Turner,	† " " "
M. Y. Johnson,	§ " " "
M. P. Silverburgh,	† " " "
Geo. G. Gould,	§ " " "
Geo. M. Mitchell,	† " " "
S. H. Helm,	† May 15, "
J. R. Scroggs,	† " "
Samuel Snider,	" "
John E. Smith,	‡ " "
T. Hallett,	" "

W. R. Rowley,	May 15th, 1858.
J. C. Spare,	May 22, "
Henry Jones,	§ " "
M. F. Burke,	§ " "
M. Faucette,	† " "
J. P. DeZoya,	‡ " ".
D. B. Morehouse,	† " "
Thos. Gooch,	§ " "
C. Klett,	" "
D. Wann,	‡ " "
Robert Fraser,	§ " "
Samuel Fraser,	§ July 17, "
J. W. Woodruff,	§ Aug. 7, "
S. O. Stillman,	" "
J. B. Slichter,	§ Aug. 21, "
E. T. Green,	§ Sept. 8, "
Wm. Spaulding,	* " 11, "
E. V. Holcomb,	§ Oct. 27, "
D. Hunkins,	§ January 5, 1859.
H. H. Gear,	‡ " 7, "
Wm. Bulger,	† February 3, "
D. D. Mills,	‖ March 25, "
H. C. Newhall,	§ May 6, "
John C. Smith,	" 21, "
A. H. LeFever,	§ July 21, "
J. S. Williams,	§ " "
John S. Marshall,	§ Aug. 5, "
Thos. J. Maupin,	§ Dec. 2, "
Geo. R. Sanford,	§ February 3, 1860.
Richard Seal,	March, 16, "

A. L. Rogers,	‖ July 6th,	1860.
J. M. Spratt,	July 28,	"
R. S. Harris,	§ Sept. 7,	"
Oliver Marble,	§ Nov. 16,	"
H. W. Foltz,	‖ ——,	"
O. M. Troxell,	† ——,	"
G. M. Conlee,	§ March 15,	1861.
John H. Conlee,	§ ——,	"
J. C. Calderwood,	June 8,	"
A. H. Davis,	§ "	"
Geo. J. Edwards,	§ Dec. 20,	"
Wm. Butler,	‖ ——,	"
Thos. R. Scott,	§ May 16,	"
Geo. W. Felt,	§ June 13th,	1862.
J. B. Young,	June 20,	"
John R. Booth,	§ July 4,	"
Richard Harvey,	§ January 2d,	1863.
B. J. Ewing,	" 16,	"
Daniel Stewart,	April 7,	"
T. R. Bird,	May, 15,	"
T. B. Farnsworth,	† ——,	"
J. W. Newburg,	§ Sept. 4,	"
Wm. H. Roberts,	§ "	"
J. S. Hunt,	‖ Dec. 6,	"
Lyman Hunt,	§ March 4th,	1864.
Benj Worden,	§ " 18,	"
Charles Semmern,	§ " 22,	"
J. K. Haines,	§ Oct. 7,	"
Wesley Jacobs,	‖ ——,	"
S. K. Miner,	——,	"

F. S. Koontz,	‖ December 2d, 1864.
J. C. Hawkins,	§ February 17, 1865.
Geo. H. Shears,	‖ April 13, "
E. A. Small,	§ " 21, "
C. P. Fox,	§ June 2, "
W. J. Fullen,	‖ " 30, "
John A. Rawlins,	† July 26, " .
W. P. Haines,	‖ Aug. 24, "
Addison Philleo,	§ October 9th, 1865.
M. M. Miller,	§ Dec. 1, "
O. L. Grant,	§ January 5th, 1866.
J. B. Parkins,	" 19, "
W. R. Holder,	Feb. 28, "
M. Coleman,	March 2, "
W. H. Kneebone,	§ Aug. 20, "
M. G. Mills,	§ Sept. 6, "
James Brown,	§ " "
John Bethel,	Nov. 2, "
Wm. Passmore,	April 19th, 1867.
Joseph Perrin,	June 7, "
J. J. Hassig,	July 5, "
Wm. James,	Aug. 2, "
Rev. C. F. Wright,	† September 6, "
James Arnott,	" 13, "
James B. Brown,	" 13, "
Thos. B. Bray,	" 20, "
Thos. Scandlyn,	" 20, "
Daniel LeBetter,	" 27, "
R. S. Raw,	Nov. 1, "
Joseph Bascom,	‖ " 15, "

August Campbell,	December 6, 1867.
Joseph Vincent,	§ January 17, 1868.
N. R. Cozzens,	Feb. 2, "
John Combellick,	‖ May 1, "
Charles F. Miller,	‖ June 19, "
C. S. Bentley,	Sept. 4, "
Wm. Spensley,	February 12, 1869.
L. T. Thomas,	§ " 12, "
S. B. Raw,	‖ " "
A. J. Louchheim,	March 5, "
Wm. R. Burkhard,	§ " 8. "
G. H. Mars,	" 8, "
L. Hassig,	§ " 12, "
Thos. Robinson,	" "
C. A. Haskel,	‖ April 3, "
J. W. Luke,	" 9, "
H. R. Bachelor,	" 9, "
C. Koontz,	" 9, "
John Thomas,	§ May 7, "
Geo. Arnott,	June 11, "
Edward James,	Sept. 17, "
Edward Courtney,	Oct. 15, "
H. H. Oldenhage,	" 21, "
Edward Jones,	§ Dec. 3, "
John A. Jones,	† " 17, "
Jacob Wernli,	March 4th, 1870.
P. Trewartha,	" 4, "
R. H. Fiddick,	Nov. 24, "
Jesse G. Crooks,	January 6, 1871.
R. J. Edwards,	" 20, "

T. G. Drenning,	April 2d,	1871.
B. F. Merten,	Jan. 20,	"
R. Weiland,	May 5,	"
W. F. Crummer,	June 23,	"
Rev. E. H. Downing,	July 7,	"
Joseph Raw,	" 7,	"
T. E. Armitstead,	§ Feb. 12th,	1872.
J. W. Wann,	" 16,	"
Theodore Burkhard,	§ " 16,	"
Sidney Hunkins,	March 4,	"
A. H. Simpson,	" 4,	"
J. D. Pryor,	§ " 11,	"
Robert Swaim,	" 11,	"
D. A. Taylor,	" 15,	"
A. V. Richards,	April 15,	"
W. H. Martin,	" 5,	"
E. G. Newhall,	" 19,	"
C. S. Merrick,	" 19,	"
L. A. Rowley,	May 1,	"
H. N. Bridgeman, Sr.	† Nov. 1,	"
J. R. Davidson,	Jan. 17th,	1873.
J. Fawcett,	Feb. 28,	"
Wm. Beadle,	§ " 7,	"
John Hatch,	March 7.	"
J. C. Glenat,	April 14,	"
Wm. Cary,	May 17,	"
R. H. Heller,	" 16,	"
H. D. Howard,	June, 19,	"
H. N. Bridgeman, Jr.	" 19,	"
D. N. Corwith,	" 19,	"

Robert Pool,	June 20th, 1873.
J. P. Williams,	June 20, "
A. F. Powell,	Oct. 17, "
Wm. H. Myers,	January 20, 1874.
Conrad Bahwell,	April 1, "
E. C. Ripley,	" 3, "
G. C. Biesmann,	" 6, "
H. F. C. Schneider,	" 6, "
H. F. Browning,	" 7, "
John Eiseman,	May 15, "
Walter Ford,	July 22, "

JO DAVIESS CHAPTER, NO. 51.

JoDaviess Chapter, No. 51, of Royal Arch Masons, was organized under Dispensation, June 9th A. D., 1859, A. S. 2389., by Deputy Grand High Priest, Comp. Wm. Mitchell.

Present, Companions Rev. E. M. Boring, of Chicago, Capt. H. H. Gear, Ely S. Parker, Geo. Thompson and M. D. Chamberlain, of Freeport, J. M. Shermerhorn, Lena, Daniel Wann, Wm. Spaulding Wm. Bulger, Dr. J. A. Scroggs, and Geo. M. Mitchell, of Galena.

After the Chapter was duly constituted, petitions were received from a number of Master Masons, acted upon and elected. From June 9th. 1859, to the present time the work of JoDaviess Chapter has been continuous, but as its history would be but a repetition of that of Miner's Lodge, we content ourselves with the By-Laws and a history of its work as shown in the list of Officers who have been called upon to preside over its destinies, and the large membership which has found companionship around its altar.

JO DAVIESS CHAPTER, NO. 51,

ROYAL ARCH MASONS.

ORGANIZED UNDER DISPENSATION,

JUNE 9TH, A. D. 1859, A. J. 2389.

CHARTER GRANTED.

NOVEMBER 24, 1859.

STATED COMMUNICATIONS

—ON—

SECOND AND FOURTH THURSDAYS

OF EACH MONTH,

In Masonic Hall, Galena, Illinois.

COPY OF CHARTER

OF

JO DAVIESS CHAPTER.

————•◆•————

THE MOST EXCELLENT GRAND ROYAL ARCH CHAPTER OF ILLINOIS.

To all whom it may concern, Send Gree'ing.--KNOW YE, "That we, the
Grand Royal Arch Chapter of Illinois, do hereby authorize and empower
our trusty and well beloved Companions, Ely S Parker, High Priest, Daniel Wann, King, George M. Mitchell, Scribe, and others, their Companions and Associates, to open and hold a Royal Arch Chapter, at the City
of Galena, by the name of JoDiviess Chapter, No. 51, and therein to
confer the several degrees of Mark Master, Past Master, Most Excellent
Master, and Royal Arch, according to the ancient customs and usages of
the craft, and not otherwise."
   "And we do further authorize and empower our said trusty and well
beloved Companions to install their successors in office, to whom they
shall deliver this Warrant of Constitution, and invest them with all their
powers and dignities as such and they in like manner their successors
in office, during the continuance of the said Royal Arch Chapter Forever.
   Provided always, That the said above named companions, and their
successors do pay and cause to be paid, due respect and obedience to the
Most Excellent Grand Royal Arch Chapter of illinois, *aforesaid*, and to
the Edicts, Rules and Regulations thereof; Otherwise this Warrant of
Constitution to be void, and of no effect.
   Given under the hands of our Grand Officers, and Seal of our Grand
Chapter, at Springfield this 30th day of September, A. D., 1859, A. L.,
5859. Y. D. 2389.

        A G. ELLWOOD, Grand High Priest
        WM. WALLACE MITCHELL, Deputy High Priest.
        A. W BLAKESLEY, Grand King.
        A. W. MOHR S. Grand Scribe.
Attest,   HARMAN G. RELNOLDS,   [SEAL.]
                Grand Secretary.

BY-LAWS.

ARTICLE I.

NAME.

This Chapter shall be known by the name of "Jo-Daviess Chapter, No. 51. Royal Arch Masons." under the jurisdiction of the Grand Chapter of Illinois.

ARTICLE II.

STATED CONVOCATIONS.

The Stated Convocations of this Chapter, shall be held on the Second and Fourth Tuesdays of each month at 7½ o'clock, P. M.

ARTICLE III.

ANNUAL CONVOCATIONS.

The Annual Convocations for the election of officers shall be held on the regular convocation next before St John's day in December, of each year.

ARTICLE IV.

ELECTIVE OFFICERS.

The M. E. High Priest,
M. E. King,
M. E. Scribe,
Secretary,
Treasurer,
Captain of Host.

Principal Sojourner, and Royal Arch Captain, shall be elected by ballot at the annual convocation of each year.

ARTICLE V.

APPOINTED OFFICERS.

Previous to the installation the M. E. High Priest shall appoint a

Grand Master of the 1st veil,
Grand Master of the 2d veil,
Grand Master of the 3d veil, and a Tyler.

ARTICLE VI.

INSTALLATION OF OFFICERS.

The Officers of this Chapter shall be installed as soon after their election as practicable, but on or before Saint John's day, Dec. 27th of each year.

ARTICLE VII.

DUTIES OF OFFICERS.

SEC. 1. The duties of the several Officers shall be such as the Constitution and Masonic traditions have settled, as well as the By-Laws of this Chapter, and the Laws and Edicts of the Grand Chapter of Illinois and the General Grand Chapter of the United States.

SEC. 2. It is incumbent on the High Priest of this Chapter, as appertaining to his office, duty and dignity, to see that the By-Laws of this Chapter, as well as the Constitution of the General Grand Chapter of the U. S. and the Regulations of the Grand Chapter of Illinois, be duly observed; that all the subordinate officers perform the duties of their respective stations faithfully, and are examples of diligence and industry to their Companions; that true and exact records be kept of all the proceedings of the Chapter by the Secretary; that the Treasurer keep and render exact and just accounts of all moneys belonging to the Chapter; that regular returns be made by the Secretary annually to the Grand Chapter, of the admission of all candidates or members; that the annual dues to the Grand Chapter be regularly and punctually paid. The Charter of the Chapter is committed to his special care and charge. He has the right and authority of calling his Chapter at pleasure, upon any emergency or occurrence which in his judgment may require their meeting, and he is to fill the chair when present.

Sec. 3. The Secretary shall keep a correct record of all the proceedings of this Chapter proper to be written. Keep accounts with all its members, make reports to the Grand Chapter when required, and make report to this Chapter at each annual convocation of its membership and of all moneys received and paid out by him during the current year together with the amounts due by the Companions, and for such duties the Secretary shall receive one dollar per night and be exempt from yearly dues.

Sec. 4. The Treasurer before entering upon the duties of his Office shall give a bond for the faithful performace and discharge of his duty, to be approv-ed by the first three officers of the Chapter, and it shall be his duty, to make report at each annual convocation of the moneys received and paid out by him.

Sec. 5. The Tyler shall take charge of the Hall, Rooms and Furniture of the Chapter, and keep them in proper order for the transaction of business and comfort of the Companions. He shall attend all Convocations of the Chapter, and serve all summons or other notices, and for such duties he shall be exempt from yearly dues and receive one dollar per night.

Sec. 6. The M. E. High Priest, King and Scribe shall be a Committee on Finance ,whose duty it shall be to examine the reports of the Secretary and Treasurer and to audit all bills presented to the Chapter.

ARTICLE VIII.

MEMBERSHIP.

Sec 1 Royal Arch Masons in good standing in a Blue Lodge in regular standing may be admitted to membership in this Chapter upon presentation of a proper Demit, and a petition in writing accompanied with a fee of Five Dollars, which petition shall be referred to a Committee of three members, who shall report at the same or the next stated Convocation, when if not elected the fee shall be returned.

PETITION FOR THE DEGREES.

Sec. 2. Each petition for the degrees in this Chapter must be in writing, accompanied with the fee of Ten Dollars, which shall be referred to a Committee of three members who shall carefully examine into the character and standing of the petitioner, and his proficiency in the first three degrees of Masonry, and report at the same or the next stated Convocation, when if not elected the fee shall be returned.

FEES FOR DEGREES.

SEC. 3. The fees for conferring the degrees of Mark Master, Past Master, Most Excellent Master and Royal Arch, shall be as follows:

For the degree of Mark Master, Ten Dollars, which shall accompany the petition.

For Past Master, Five Dollars.

For Most Excellent Master, Five Dollars,

For Royal Arch, Ten Dollars.

Which sums shall be severally paid at or before the time of taking each degree.

SEC. 4. Each member shall sign these By-Laws on the night of his admission on Demit, or Exhaltation; and no one shall be entitled to a vote until he has signed said Laws

ARTICLE IX.

ANNUAL DUES.

Each member of this Chapter shall pay into the Treasury the sum of Two dollars per annum, which shall include the Grand Chapter dues, and shall be due on the first day of January of each year, and payable before the annual Convocation; and any member indebted to this Chapter shall not be entitled to vote, and ineligible to any Office, and if in arrears for one year, he may be suspended after due notice and trial, unless by a unanimous vote of the Chapter he be exempted from payment of said arrearages.

ARTICLE X.

DEMITS.

A Demit may be granted to any member (except an elective Officer,) who may have moved without the jurisdiction of this Chapter, or for the purpose of petitioning for a new Chapter, provided he be in good standing and not indebted to the Chapter.

ARTICLE XI.

DISCIPLINE AND JURISDICTION.

Sec. 1. A regular charge in writing, specifying the nature of the offense, and signed by the accuser shall be delivered to the Secretary, who shall read it at the next regular Convocation, at which time the Most Excellent High Priest shall appoint the time for trial, of which it shall be the duty of the Secretary to give due and timely notice to the accused, who shall be entitled to a copy of the charges, and to ample time and opportunity to prepare his defense.

Sec. 2. All trials shall be in the highest degree to which the accused has attained, and the examination of witnesses shall take place in the presence of both the accused and accuser, whether in the Chapter, or before a Committee.

Sec. 3. The form and manner of trial shall be the same as that laid down by the Grand Lodge of Illinois for the government of its Subordinate Lodges, where the same does not conflict with any law, edict or usage of the Grand Royal Arch Chapter of this State.

Sec. 4. This Chapter may exercise disciplinary jurisdiction over all Royal Arch Masons, and Masons of any of the dependant degrees, residing within its jurisdiction, *Provided*, That in all cases of discipline, the accused shall have the same rights, and the same rules be observed as are prescribed for members of this Chapter, and by the usages of the Order.

SEC. 5. If a member be expelled from this Chapter, the Secretary shall forthwith notify the Grand Chapter thereof, and such other Masonic Bodies as the nature of the case may require.

ARTICLE XII.

BY-LAWS AND RULES.

SEC. 1. These By-Laws, together with all ordinances, rules, orders and regulations passed by this Chapter, shall be observed in the Lodges of the dependent degrees, as far as the same are applicable.

SEC. 2. No alteration, addition or amendment shall be made to these By-Laws unless proposed in writing, and read at a stated meeting, and shall not then be acted upon until the second stated meeting thereafter, when it shall require a vote of two-thirds of the members present for its adoption, unless directed to do so by the Grand Chapter, to conform to the regulations of the Grand Chapter of this State, or of the General Grand Chapter of the United States.

ORDER OF BUSINESS:

1. Reading of Record.
2. Reading and Referring Petitions.
3. Reports of Committees on Petitions.
4. Balloting on Petitions.
5. Miscellaneous Business.
6. Work.

OFFICERS AND MEMBERS.

OFFICERS—1859.

Ely S. Parker,	High Priest.
Daniel Wann,	King.
Geo. M. Mitchell,	Scribe.
John E. Smith,	C. H.
Wm. Spaulding,	P. S.
W. R. Rowley,	R. A. C.
Darius Hunkins,	G. M., 1st V.
Jonathan W. Woodruff,	G. M., 2d V.
John A. Scroggs,	G. M.. 3d V.
Madison Y. Johnson,	Treas.
S. O. Stillman,	Sec.
M. Faucette,	Tyler.

OFFICERS—1860.

Ely S. Parker,	High Priest.
Wm. Spaulding,	King.
Daniel Wann,	Scribe.
John E. Smith,	C. H.
D. D. Mills,	P. S.
M. Y. Johnson,	R. A. C.
D. Hunkins,	G. M., 1st V.
J. W. Woodruff,	G. M., 2d V.

J. S. Williams,	G. M., 3d V.
W. R. Rowley,	Treas.
S. O. Stillman,	Sec.
M. Faucette,	Tyler.

OFFICERS—1861.

Ely S. Parker,	High Priest.
D. Hunkins,	King.
M. Y. Johnson,	Scribe.
John E. Smith,	C. H.
J. S. Williams,	P. S.
E. T. Green,	R. A. C.
Samuel Fraser,	G. M., 1st V.
J. W. Woodruff,	G. M., 2d V.
G. M. Mitchell,	G. M., 3d V.
W. R. Rowley,	Treas.
S. O. Stillman,	Sec.
M. Faucette,	Tyler.

OFFICERS—1862.

D. Hunkins,	High Priest.
M. Y. Johnson,	King.
H. H. Gear,	Scribe.
Geo. M. Mitchell,	C. H.
J. C. Smith,	R. A. C.
J. S. Williams,	P. S.
J. M. Spratt,	G. M., 3d V.
J. W. Woodruff,	G. M., 2d V.
Samuel Fraser,	G. M., 1st V.
D. Wann,	Treas.
S. O. Stillman,	Sec.
M. Faucette,	Tyler.

111

Samuel Snider,	High Priest.
M. Y. Johnson,	King.
D. B. Morehouse,	Scribe.
Geo. M. Mitchell,	C. H.
E. T. Green,	R. A. C.
J. M. Spratt,	G. M., 3d V.
R. S. Harris,	G. M., 2d V.
J. R. Booth,	G. M., 1st V.
D. Wann,	Treas.
S. O. Stillman,	Sec.
M. Faucette,	Tyler.

OFFICERS.— 1864.

Samuel Snider,	High Priest.
D. Wann.	King.
D. B. Morehouse,	Scribe.
Geo. M. Mitchell,	C. H.
S. Fraser,	P. S.
E. T. Green,	R. A. C.
O. Marble,	G. M., 3d V.
S. K. Miner,	G. M., 2d V.
J. M. Spratt,	G. M., 1st V.
S. O. Stillman,	Sec. and Treas.
M. Faucette,	Tyler.

OFFICERS—1865.

Saml. Snider,	High Priest.
D. Wann,	King.
N. F. Wobb,	Scribe.
Geo. M. Mitchell	C. H.

O. Marble,	P. S.
E. T. Green,	R. A. C.
J. M. Spratt,	G. M., 3d V.
S. K. Miner,	G. M., 2d V.
J. B. Young,	G. M., 1st V.,
S. O. Stillman,	Sec. and Treas.
M. Faucette,	Tyler.

OFFICERS.—1866.

Saml. Snider,	High Priest.
D. Wann,	King.
N. F. Webb,	Scribe.
T. R. Bird,	C. H.
J. A. Scroggs.	P. S.
J. M. Spratt,	R . A. .
S. K. Miner,	G. M., 3d V.
A. L. Rogers,	G. M., 2d V.
Geo. F. Shears,	G. M., 1st V.
S. O. Stillman,	Sec. and Treas.
O. Marble,	Tyler.

OFFICERS.—1867.

Saml. Snider,	High Priest.
D. Wann,	King.
E. A. Small	Scribe.
T. R. Bird,	C. H.
E. T. Green,	P. S.
J. M. Spratt,	R. A. C.
S. K. Miner,	G. M. 3d V.
J. C. Spare,	G. M. 2d V.
G. F. Shears,	G. M. 1st V.
S. O. Stillman,	Sec. and Treas.
Charles Semmern,	Tyler.

OFFICERS.—1868.

John C. Smith,	High Priest.
D. Wann,	King.
E. A. Small,	Scribe.
T. R. Bird,	C. H.
B. J. Ewing,	P. S.
J. M. Spratt,	R. A. C.
S. K. Miner,	G. M., 3d V.
D. Stewart,	G. M., 2d V.
S. Fraser,	G. M , 1st V.
S. O. Stillman,	Sec. and Treas
Chas. Semmern,	Tyler.

OFFICERS.—1869.

J. C. Smith,	High Priest.
D. Stewart,	King.
S. K. Miner,	Scribe.
T. R. Bird,	C. H.
B. J. Ewing,	P. S.
J. M. Spratt,	R. A. C.
J. J. Hassig,	G. M., 3d V.
J. B. Young,	G. M., 2d V.
S. Fraser,	G. M., 1st V.
S. O. Stillman,	Sec. and Treas.
Chas. Semmern,	Tyler.

OFFICERS.—1870.

J. C. Smith,	High Priest.
D. Stewart,	King.
D. LeBetter,	Scibe.
T. R. Bird,	C. H.
S. O. Stillman,	P. S.

J. M. Spratt,	R. A. C.
W. Jacobs,	G. M., 3d V.
J. B. Brown,	G. M., 2d V.
S. K. Miner,	G. M., 1st V.
S. O. Stillman,	Sec. and Treas.
F. S. Koontz,	Tyler.

OFFICERS.—1871.

J. C. Smith,	High Priest.
D. LeBetter,	King.
J. Wernli,	Scribe.
J. M. Spratt,	C. H.
S. O. Stillman,	P. S.
M. Coleman,	R. A. C.
A. J. Louchheim,	G. M., 3d V.
W. R. Burkhard,	G. M., 2d V.
S. K. Miner,	G. M., 1st V.
S. O. Stillman,	Sec. and Treas.
D. Stewart,	Tyler,

OFFICERS.—1872.

John C. Smith,	High Priest.
D. LeBetter,	King.
J. Wernli,	Scribe.
J. M. Spratt,	C. H.
H. H. Oldenhage,	P. S.
M. Coleman,	R. A. C.
R. H. Fiddick,	G. M., 3d V.
W. R. Burkhard,	G. M., 2d V.
S. K. Miner,	G. M., 1st V.
S. O. Stillman,	Sec. and Treas.
D. Stewart,	Tyler.

OFFICERS.—1873.

J. C. Smith,	High Priest.
S. K. Miner,	King.
J. Wernli,	Scribe.
D. LeBetter,	C. H.
C. S. Bentley,	P. S.
J. C. Calderwood,	R. A. C.
R. H. Fiddick,	G. M., 3d V.
M. Coleman,	G. M., 2d V.
T. E. Armitstead,	G. M., 1st V.
J. M. Spratt,	Treas.
S. O. Stillman,	Sec.
D. Stewart,	Tyler,

OFFICERS.—1874.

J. C. Smith,	High Priest.
S. K. Miner,	King.
R. H. Fiddick,	Scribe.
J. M. Spratt,	Treas.
D. LeBetter,	Sec.
J. Fawcett,	C. H.
C. S. Bentley,	P. S.
J. R. Davidson,	R. A. C.
J. P. Williams,	G. M., 3d V.
H. N. Bridgeman, Jr.	G. M., 2d V.
A. M. Powell,	G. M., 1st V.
D. Stewart,	Tyler.

MEMBERS ADMITTED ON DEMIT AND EXALTED.

Ely S. Parker,	† June	9th.	1859
D. Wann,	"	9,	"

Geo. M. Mitchell,	†	June 9,	1859
Wm. Spaulding,	‖	" 9,	"
H. H. Gear,	‡	" 9,	"
Wm. Bulger,	†	" 9,	"
John A. Scroggs,	†	" 9,	"
J. W. Woodruff,	§	" 11,	"
M. Y. Johnson,	§	" 11,	"
W. R. Rowley,		" 11,	"
S. O. Stillman,		" 11,	"
D. Hunkins, .	§	" 11,	"
John E. Smith,	‡	" 22	"
D. B. Morehouse,	†	" 22	"
M. Faucette,	†	" 22	"
W. Foster,	§	July 25	"
D. D. Mills,	§	" 25	"
J. S. Williams,	§	Dec. 1,	"
Samuel Fraser,	§	" 1,	"
N F. Webb,	†	———	"
E. T. Green,	§	March 15th.	1860.
J. C. Smith,		" 15,	"
R. H. Harris,	§	March 19th.	1861.
Jas. M. Spratt,		" 19,	"
S. K. Miner,		19,	"
Saml. Snider,		July 31st,	1862.
J. R. Booth,	§	" 31,	"
Oliver Marble,	§	" 31,	"
James B. Young,	§	Dec. 30th,	1863.
T. R. Bird,		" 30,	"
Wesley Jacobs	‖	" 30,	"
W. H. Roberts,	§	Nov. 25,	1864.

R. E. Odell,	Feby. 10th, 1865.
M. Marvin,	‖ " 10, "
J. C. Calderwood,	" 10, "
Geo. J. Edwards,	§ July 14, "
A. L. Rogers,	‖ " 14, "
Geo. G. Shears,	§ Aug. 1, "
M. Maynard,	" 1, "
T. R. Scott,	§ " 1, "
E. A. Small,	§ Jan. 12th, 1866.
J. C. Spare,	" 12, "
A. H. Davis,	§ " 12, "
A. Reynolds,	June 8, "
Henry Glessner,	" 8, "
John Weber,	" 8, "
R. S. Martin,	Sept. 28, "
D. Stewart,	28, "
C. P. Fox,	28, "
J. P. Black,	Nov. 9, "
J. C. Robbins,	§ " 9, "
H. J. D. Maynard,	" 9, "
Geo. Marshall,	March 8th, 1867.
B. J. Ewing,	" 8, "
Chas. Semmern,	§ " 8, "
John Bethel,	April 26, "
Edward James,	" 26, "
J. B. Parkins,	" 26, "
Rev. N. F Wright,	† June 29th, 1868.
J. B. Brown,	" 29, "
J. J. Hassig,	" 29, "

Cas. S Burt,	July 9th, 1868
A. H. Moody,	" 9, "
B. Worden,	" 9, "
John Goldthorp,	April 29th, 1839
N. R. Cozzens,	" 29, "
J. H. Bascom,	‖ " 29, "
John Combellick,	‖ June 3d, "
Danl. LeBetter,	" 3, "
C. S. Bentley,	" 3, "
Thos. E. Moore,	Jan. 27th, 1870.
Joseph Perrin,	" 27, "
John NeCollins,	" 27, "
Samuel Cook,	† Feb. 17, "
N. M. Bratt,	" 17 "
F. S. Koontz,	‖ " 17, "
Jacob Wernli,	May, 26, "
Rev. S. A. W. Jewett,	‡ March 12, "
M. Coleman,	" 12, '
W. R. Burkhard,	§ " 12, "
John Creighton,	June 9, "
J. B. Chapman,	" 9, "
A. J. Louchheim,	" 9, "
Frank Campbell,	Sept. 22, "
J. W. White,	January 26, 1871.
Stephen Jeffers,	" 26, "
John Olinger,	" 26, "
J. G. Crooks,	March 9, "
H. H. Oldenhage,	" 9, "
R. H. Fiddick,	" 9, "
B. F. Merten,	March 30, "

P. Trewartha,	March	30th,	1871.
R. J. Edwards,	"	30,	"
J. S. Higgins,	May	25,	"
N. P. Marton,	"	25,	"
J. D. Clise,	"	25,	"
J. W. Luke,	Dec.	5,	".
W. R. Holder,	"	5,	"
W. F. Crummer,	"	5,	"
Theo. Burkhard,	§ March	29th,	1872.
Sidney Hunkins,	"	29,	"
W. H. Martin,	"	29,	"
Rev. E. H. Downing,	‡ April	25,	"
T. E. Armitstead,	§ "	25,	"
J. D. Pryor,	§ "	25,	"
Edward Courtney,	May	30,	"
L. A. Rowley,	"	30,	"
Wm. Cary,	"	30.	"
D. A. Taylor,	February	3d,	1873.
C. S. Merrick,	"	3,	"
J. R. Davidson,	"	3,	"
Rev. Joseph Crummer,	‡ March 27,		"
Jacob Fawcett,	" 27,		"
A. V. Richards,	" 27,		"
M. J. Draper,	April 1,		"
Levi Johnson,	" 1,		"
E. G. Newhall,	" 1,		"
G. H. Mars,	May 22,		"
John Hatch,	" 22,		"
J. C. Glenat,	" 22,		"
H. D. Howard,	July 22,		"

H . N. Bridgeman, Jr.	July 22d,	1873.
John P. Williams,	" 22,	"
John E. Hoover,	Aug. 14,	"
D . N. Corwith,	Nov. 18,	"
R. H. Heller,	" 18,	"
A . F. Powell,	" 18,	"
H. N. Bridgman, Sr.	† Dec. 9,	"
Robert Robson,	" 9,	"
James Carr,	" 9,	"
Wm. Spensley,	January 8th,	1874.
R . M. Spensley,	" 8,	"
H. R. Bachelor,	" 8,	"
James Allen,	April 23,	"
E. C. Ripley,	" 23,	"
C. Bahwell,	" 23,	"
H. C. F. Schneider,	May 18,	"
Geo. C. Biesmann,	. " 18,	"
Robert Pool,	" 18,	"

ELY S. PARKER COUNCIL, No. 60.

Ely S. Parker Council, No. 60, was constituted un
der a Dispensation from the Thrice Illustrious George
E. Loumsburg, Grand Puissant of the Grand Council of Illinois, July 9th, 1873, and is duly authorized
to confer the degrees of Royal, Super Excellent and
Select Master's degrees, the eighth, ninth and tenth
degrees of the Ancient York Rite. The history of
this Council is brief, named after the first Master of
Miners' Lodge and High Priest of Jo Daviess Chapter, Gen. Ely S. Parker, the talented Indian Chief,
a grandson of Red Jacket, whose history every read-
er of American events is familiar with, now the present Chief of the Six Nations. It was to be expected
that the constituting of this body would draw together a large number of prominent Masons. The expec-
tation was fully realized, as the following notice of the
event taken from the daily papers fully show :

"Wednesday, July 9th, was a grand gala day for the brethren of the
Mystic Tie, of this city. The event being the organization of a Council
of Cryptic Masonry, an occasion which brought to our city many distin-
guished alike in civil life and eminent in Masonry. Among these were
Hon H. C. Burchard, M. C., Gen. Smith D. Atkins, Hon. Rob't Little,
W. S. Best, L. L. Munn, Jas. S. McCall, C. H. Hutchinson, W. D. Row-
ell, W. O. Wright, F. Kindinger, J. S. Gates, and S. K. Schofield all of
Freeport Council No. 39.

The Craft were called to labor at 8 P. M., by Comp. J. C. Smith, the following Companions presiding:

W. S. Best—Thrice Illustrious Grand Master.
L. L. Munn—Deputy Illustrious Grand Master.
James S. McCall—Principal Con. of Work.
C. H. Hutchison—Captain of Guards.
Robert Little—Recorder.

After the work of constituting was completed the following well known Galena Masons were inducted into the Cryptic Rite:

Gen. W. R. Rowley,   S. O. Stillman,   S. K. Miner.   R. H. Fiddick,
J. C. Calderwood,   J. Fawcett,   C. S. Bentley,   G. H. Mars,
A. J. Lonchheim,   Sidney Hunkins,   A. H. Moody,   Daniel Stewart,
Daniel LeBetter,   M. Coleman,   J. M. Spratt.   W. R. Holder.

The Craft continued at labor until the "wee sma hours ayant the twae," when, after addresses appropriate to the occasion by Companions J. C Smith, L. L. Munn, James Mc 'all and others, the Craft were called from labor to refreshment, when amid a 'a flow of reason" and an interchange of Masonic sentiments, the brethren disbanded, well pleased with the occasion, which called them together.

' Ely S. Parker Council" is named after the eminent Mason, Gen. Parker, late Commissioner of Indian Affairs, and the first W. M. of Miners' Lodge and H. P. of JoDaviess Chapter of this city.

Galena Masons are known throughout this and other jurisdictions as thorough workers, and may well feel proud of having *all* the Masonic Bodies in this city fully officered and in complete working order to confer all the degrees of the Ancient and Accepted York Rite, which are as follows:

Miners' Lodge, No. 273, A. F. and A. M.
Jo Daviess Chapter, No. 51 R. A. M.
Ely S. Parker Council, U. D., (now No. 60.)
Galena Commandery, No. 40, Knights Templars.

The above named bodies are under the charge of that well known Masonic worker, D. D. G. M., Gen. J. C. Smith, who has the distinguished honor conferred upon him of having received *all* the Masonic degrees of the York and Scottish Rites of Masonry."

BY-LAWS

—OF—

ELY S. PARKER COUNCIL No. 60.

Royal, Super-Excellent and Select Masters.

ORGANIZED UNDER DISPENSATION FROM THE THRICE
ILLUSTRIOUS GEORGE E. LOUMSBURY, GRAND
PUISSANT OF THE GRAND COUNCIL OF
ILLINOIS, JULY 9th, 1873.

DISPENSATION DATED MAY 26th, 1873.

CHARTER GRANTED BY THE GRAND COUNCIL OF ILLI-
NOIS, OCTOBER 29th, 1873.

Stated Conventions

THE FIRST MONDAY

OF EACH MONTH,

In Masonic Hall, Galena, Illinois.

ELY S. PARKER COUNCIL NO. 60.

"I am Alpha and Omega."

FROM THE CENTRE OF THE GRAND COUNCIL OF ROYAL AND SELECT
MASTERS OF THE STATE OF ILLINOIS.

To All and Every, our Illustrious Companions, Send Greeting—KNOW
YE, That at the Petition of our Illustrious and Beloved Companions,
John C. Smith, Simeon K. Miner, Mahlon Coleman, Daniel LeBetter,
John C. Calderwood, Charles S. Bentley, Daniel Stewart, William R
Holder, Richard H. Fiddick, Amasa H. Moody, Sidney Huukins, Jacob Faw
cett, Samuel O. Stillman, James M. Spratt, Gerhard H. Mars. and A. J
Louchhiem, residing at or near Galena, in the County of Jo Daviess, and
State of Illinois, do hereby constitute the said Companions into a Reg-
ular Council of Royal and Select Masters, to be opened at the aforesaid
Galena, by the name of Ely S. Parker Council No. 60. And do further
at the said Petition, and the great trust and confidence reposed in the
above named Companions, hereby appoint John C. Smith, Thrice Illustrious Grand Master, Richard H. Fiddick, Deputy Illustrious Grand
Master, Jacob Fawcett, Principal Conductor of the Work, for opening
the said Council, and for such time only as may be thought proper by
the Companions thereof. It being my will that said appointments shall in
no case affect any future election of Officers of the Council, but that the
same shall be according to the Regulations of the Council, and consistent with the General Laws of the Society, contained in the Book of
Constitutions And (d) hereby require you, the said John C. Smith, to
take special care that all and every, the said Companions are or have
been, regularly made Royal, Select and Super Excellent Masters; and
that they do perform and observe and keep all the rules and orders contained in the Book of Constitutions, also such as may from time to time
be transmitted to them from the Grand Council, and further, That you
do, from time to time cause to be entered in a book kept for that purpose
an account of your proceedings in the Council, together with such regulations as shall be made for the good government thereof, a copy of
which you are in nowise to omit laying before the Grand Council once in
each year, together with a list of the members of the Council. That
you annually pay into the Grand Treasury, such sums as may be required of you toward the Grand Council Fund, and moreover I hereby will
and do require of you the said John C. Smith, as soon as conveniently
may be, to send an account in writing, of what shall be done by virtue
of these presents.

Given at Chicago, under my hand and Seal of Masonry, this twenty-
ninth day of October, A. Dep. 2873, A. D. 1873.

Signed, GEO. E. LOUNSBURG,

Thrice Ill. Grand Puissant,

Attested, James H. Miles, [SEAL.]
Grand Recorder.

MEMBERS UNDER DISPENSATION.

Companion John Corson Smith.
"   Loyal L. Munn.
"   Wm. Young.
"   L. J. Turner.
"   Robert Little.
"   W. J. McKinn.
"   J. S. Gates.
"   E. C. Warner.
"   George Thompson.
"   James S. McCall.

OFFICERS APPOINTED BY GRAND PUIS-SANT.

Gen. John C. Smith, Thrice Ills. Grand Master, Robert Little, Deputy Ills. Grand Master, Loyal L. Munn, Prin. Con. of the work.

BY-LAWS.

ARTICLE I.

NAME.

The name of this Council shall be " Ely S, Parker No. 60, " under the jurisdiction of the Grand Council of Illinois.

ARTICLE II.

STATED CONVENTIONS.

The stated conventions of this Council shall be the first Monday in each month, at 7½ o'clock P. M.

ARTICLE III.

ANNUAL CONVENTIONS.

The annual convention for the election of officers shall be held on the first Monday in December of each year.

ARTICLE IV.

ELECTIVE OFFICERS.

The Thrice Illustrious Grand Master, Deputy Illustrious Grand Master, Principal Conductor of the Work, Recorder and Treasurer, shall be elected by ballot, at the annual Convention of each year.

ARTICLE V.

OFFICERS APPOINTED.

Previous to the Installation the Thrice Illustrious Grand Master shall appoint a Chaplain, Captain of the Guards, Conductor of the Council, Steward, and Sentinel.

ARTICLE VI.

INSTALLATION OF OFFICERS.

The Installation of the Officers shall take place as soon after the election as is convenient, but on or before Saint John's day, December 27th, of each year.

ARTICLE VII.

DUTIES OF OFFICERS.

The duties of the several Officers shall be in accordance with the Ancient Landmarks of Cryptic Masonry, the work, Ritual and Laws of the Grand Council of Illinois.

ARTICLE VIII.

BOND OF TREASURER.

Before entering upon the duties of his office, the Treasurer shall give a bond for the faithful performance and discharge of his duty, to be approved by the first three Officers of the Council.

ARTICLE IX.

ANNUAL REPORTS OF RECORDER AND TREASURER.

At each annual Convention the Recorder and Treasurer shall render an account of all moneys received and paid out by them, respectively, for the current year.

ARTICLE X.

FINANCE COMMITTEE.

The Thrice Illustrious G. M., Deputy Illustrious G. M., and P. C. of the Work, shall be a Committee on Finance, whose duty it shall be to examine the reports of the Recorder and Treasurer, and all bills shall be referred to and examined by them.

ARTICLE XI.

RECORDER AND SENTINEL.

The Recorder and Sentinel shall each receive one dollar for each night's services.

ARTICLE XII.

FEES FOR DEGREES.

The fees for conferring the degrees of Royal, Super-Excellent, and Select Master shall be ten dollars, which amount shall be paid on presentation of Petition, or before conferring said degrees.

ARTICLE XIII.

DUES.

No dues will be collected by this Council unless there are no funds in the Treasury, when an assessment will be made *pro. rata*, to pay whatever liability the Council may have incurred.

ARTICLE XIV.

DEMIT.

A Demit may be granted to any member (except

the elective Officers,) upon application at a stated Convention, and on a majority vote of the members of the Council present.

ARTICLE ·XV.

AMENDMENTS TO BY-LAWS.

Any amendment to these By-Laws shall be presented in writing at a stated Convention, and lie over one month, when a two-thirds vote of all the members present shall be necessary to the adoption of any such amendment.

ORDER OF BUSINESS:

1. Reading of Records.
2. Reading and Referring Petitions.
3. Reports of Committees on Petitions.
4. Balloting on Petitions.
5. Miscellaneous Business.
6. Work.

OFFICERS, A. D. 1873, A. Dep. 2373.

Comp, John C. Smith,   Thrice Ill. Grand Master.
"   Robert Little,   Deputy Ill. Grand Master.
"   Loyal L. Munn,   Prin. Con. of the Work
"   Gerhard H. Mars,   Chaplain.
"   Daniel LeBetter,   Recorder.
"   Richard H. Fiddick Treasurer.
"   Jacob Fawcette,   Conducter.
"   Simeon K. Miner, Capt. of Guards.
"   Abraham J. Louchheim, Steward.
"   Daniel Stewart,   Sentinel.

OFFICERS UNDER CHARTER 1873-4, A. DE-
POSIT. 2873-4.

Comp John C. Smith,   Thrice Ill. Grand Master.
"   Richard H. Fiddick, Deputy Ill. Grand Master.
"   Jacob Fawcett,   Prin. Con. of the Work.
"   G· H. Mars,   Chaplain.
"   D. LeBetter,   Recorder.
"   A. J. Louchheim,   Treasurer.
"   J. P. Williams,   ·Conductor.
"   J R Davidson,   Capt. Guards.
"   D. Stewart,   Steward and Sentinel.

Companions at date of Constituting Council, and chosen to the Circle of Perfection since.

§ Demitted.

MEMBERS ON DISPENSATION.

✓ Comp. John C. Smith,
"   Loyal L. Munn,   §
"   Robert Little,   §
"   William Young,   §
"   L. J. Turner,   §
"   W. J. McKim,   §
"   J. S. Gates,   §
"   E. C. Warner,   §
"   George Thompson,   §
"   James S. McCall,   §

		When Chosen.
Comp.	John C. Smith,	Feby. 19th, 1873.
"	William R. Rowley,	July 9 "
"	Simeon K. Miner,	" 9 "
"	Mahlon Coleman,	" 9 "
"	Daniel LeBetter,	" 9 "
"	John C. Calderwood,	" · 9 "
"	Charles S. Bentley,	" 9 "
"	Daniel Stewart,	" 9 "
"	Wm. R. Holder,	" 9 "

Comp.	Richard H. Fiddick,	July 9th, 1873	
"	Amase H. Moody,	" 9,	"
"	Sidney Hunkins,	" 9,	"
"	Jacob Fawcette,	" 9,	"
"	Samuel O. Stillman,	" 9,	"
"	James M. Spratt,	" 9,	"
"	Gerhart H. Mars,	" 9,	"
"	Abraham J. Louchheim,	" 9,	"
"	Benjamin F. Merten,	Aug. 13.	"
"	Jacob R. Davidson,	" 13,	"
"	Charles S. Merrick,	" 13,	"
"	Horatio N. Bridgeman, Jr.	" 18,	"
"	John W. Luke,	" 18,	"
"	John P. Williams,	" 18,	"
"	John E. Hoover,	" 25,	"
"	John S. Wiley,	" 25,	"
"	W. H. Harrison,	Sept. 7,	"
"	N. H. Brown,	Nov. 10,	"
"	H. D. Howard,.	" 28,	"
"	J. B. Brown,	" 28,	"
"	D. A. Taylor,	" 28,	"
"	D. N. Corwith,	" 28,	"
"	T. E. Armitstead,	" 28,	"
"	J. G. Crooks,	Dec. 1st.	"
"	W. H. Martin,	" 1,	"
"	J. C. Glenat,	" 1,	"
"	E. H. Downing,	" 1,	"
"	Hiram Tyrrell,	" 8th,	"
"	John Hatch,	" 8	"

Comp.	Richard Heller,	Dec. 10th, 1873.	
"	Peter Trewartha,	" 10,	"
"	W . F . Crummer,	" 15,	"
"	E . James,	" 15,	"
"	S . Jeffers,	Jany. 8th, 1874.	
"	J . W. White,	" 8,	"
"	Thos . S. Moore,	" 8,	"
"	A . Reynolds,	" 8,	"
"	R . M. Spensley,	Feb. 19th	"
"	James Cary,	" 19,	"
"	Robert Robson,	" 19,	"
"	M . M . Wheeler,	March 2d,	"
"	S . D . Pryor,	" 2,	"
"	E. C . Ripley,	May 4th,	"
"	A. V . Richards,	" 4,	"
"	C. Bahwell,	" 4,	"
"	James Allen,	June 1,	"
"	H. C. F. Schneider,	" 1,	"
"	Geo. C. Biesmann,	" 1,	"

GALENA COMMANDERY No. 40, KNIGHTS TEMPLARS.

This Body, duly authorized to confer the Chival-
rous Orders of Knights of the Red Cross, Knights
Templars, and Knights of Malta, was duly organized
Sept. 29, 1871.

Owing to the absence from home of the R. E. Grand
Commander, John M. Rierson, the Deputy Grand
Commander, Wiley M. Egan, issued his Dispensation bearing date Sept. 19, 1871, under which the
Body was convened, and such was their work that the
Grand Commandery was justified in granting a regular Charter at its Session which convened the next
month. What was done at the constituting of this
body is best told in the language of a writer of that
day. What was expected of this Chivalrous organization and what has been done, its work will attest:

"GALENA COMMANDERY, U. D."

" While Galena has for many years had a flourish-
ing Blue Lodge of Masons, and a Royal Arch Chapter
there has been no Commandery here. There being
several Sir Knights in the County, and others wishing
to receive the Orders, measures were taken to es-

tablish a Commandery in Galena, and the project was brought to a successful issue. The first regular conclave of the Commandery was held last Friday, at Masonic Hall, under the charge of the officers previously appointed: Gen. John C. Smith, Eminent Commander, Samuel Cook, Generalissimo, and Simeon K. Miner, Captain General. There were present not less than forty distinguished Sir Knights from abroad, to assist in conferring the Orders of Knighthood. There were about twenty-five from Freeport, among whom we noticed Past Grand Commander Dr. N. F. Prentice, Hon. H. C. Burchard, M. C., Gen. Smith D. Atkins, Hon. E. L. Cronkrite, Mayor of Freeport, Dr. W. J. McFlim, Robert Little, U. S. Collector, James S. McCall, Capt. Young, and others. From Dunleith there were Hon. Samuel Cook, Hon. John Ohnger, Homer Graves, and Capt. J. M. Daggett, while Dubuque was represented by about twelve Knights, Past Deputy Grand Commander Horace Tuttle and Dr. W. P. Allen being in charge. Sir James J. Peck, of Iowa City, and others from a distance were also present.

"The Commandery was opened at 3 o'clock P. M., continuing in session until 6 o'clock next morning, except during the brief recesses for refreshment. Orders were conferred upon the following named Companions: Gen. W. R. Rowley, Daniel Stewart, M. Coleman, Daniel LeBetter, J. C. Calderwood, and W. R. Burkhard. P. G. Commander Prentice and P.

D. G. Commander Tuttle conferring the Orders, with Dr. Allen as Prelate.

"At nine o'clock in the evening a recess was called, and the Sir Knights in full uniform, proceeded to the residence of Mr. L. S. Felt, to pay their respects to President Grant. They were as fine looking a body of men as ever paraded our streets. The President received them cordially, and after all had shaken hands with him, they returned to their Asylum to resume work.

"At 12 o'clock the hour for refreshments having arrived, the Sir Knights repaired to Owens' Hall, where a fine banquet had been prepared. At the close of the banquet, work was resumed, and continued till the hour of departure of the trains next morning.

"The Commandery starts out with flattering prospects, and its firs t Conclave was a pleasant one to all concerned."

Since the above was written more than fifty Companions have been created and dubbed with the Chivalrous orders of Christian Masonry. The Commandery has been called upon to attend two Templar funerals: That of Sir Knight W. D. Putnam, of Warren, and the early and warm friend of our Commandery, Past Grand Commander Dr. N. F. Prentice, of Freeport, each of whom were buried with Knightly honors, at the place of their late residence.

On the 15th day of June, 1874, the occasion of laying the Corner Stone of the new Public Hall, and the Dedication of the new Masonic building, Galena Commandery was out in full force numbering over thirty swords, and "under the command of Generalissimo Sir W. R. Rowley, assisted by Capt. Gen. Sir C. S. Bentley, excited the admiration of the spectators for the rapidity with which they executed the various Templar movements in passing from columns of three to that of the Passion Cross and several other movements known to Templar Masonry."

Fraters, our labors are ended. We have not intended, nor did you expect, when you requested that we rescue from oblivion the names of the early workers in Masonry in this city, that we would give you a treatise on the Mystic brotherhood, but that we would look up the "Old Records," seek out the names of all connected with the Craft, and place them with the By-Laws of the present bodies in one book, that each and every Galena Mason might the better trace his genealogy (Masonic history) from the organization of the first Lodge, "Strangers' Union," to the present day.

If we have succeeded in doing this with a reasonable degree of accuracy, and have met your expectations, we are amply recompensed, and will close our labors in the firm knowledge that the Galena Masons have done what it behooves every Masonic body to do— to put their work on record that it may be in the hands of every member.

We would, therefore, fraternally and courteously bid you an affectionate Farewell.

BY-LAWS

OF

Galena Commandery

NO. 40,

OF

KNIGHTS TEMPLARS,

AND

THE APPENDANT ORDERS.

Organized under Dispensation from Wiley M. Egan, Deputy Grand Commander
of the Grand Commandery of Illinois, Sept. 29th, 1871.

DISPENSATION GRANTED · SEPT 19, 1871,

Charter Granted by Grand Commandery of Illinois, Oct. 24, 1871.

STATED CONCLAVES

THE FIRST THURSDAY OF EACH MONTH,

IN MASONIC HALL, GALENA. ILL,

Members under Dispensation.

Sir John Corson Smith, ✓
Sir Samuel Cook,
Sir Simeon Kingsley Miner,
Sir John Minott Daggett,
Sir Mortimer Marcus Wheeler,
Sir John Olinger, - ✓
Sir Charles Silas Burt,
Sir Robert Little,
Sir Smith D. Atkins. ✓

Officers appointed by Grand Commander.

E. Sir John Corson Smith,—*Eminent Commander.* ✓
Sir Samuel Cook,—*Generalissimo*.
Sir Simeon Kingsley Miner,—*Captain General.*

COPY OF CHARTER

OF

GALENA COMMANDERY.

THE GRAND COMMANDERY OF KNIGHTS TEMPLARS OF THE STATE OF ILLINOIS.

To whom it may concern,—Greeting;
WHEREAS, HERETOFORE, TO-WIT:—On the nine'eenth day of September, in the year of our Lord, One Thousand Eight Hundred and Seventy-one, a Dispensation was granted to Sir John Corson Smith, Simeon Kingsley Miner, Mahlon Coleman, Mortimer Marcus Wheeler, William Rudolph Burkhard, William Reuben Rowley, John Carter Calderwood, Daniel LeBetter, and Daniel Stewart, to open and hold a Commandery of Knights Templars and the Appendant Orders, in the City of Galena, in the County of Jo Daviess, and State of Illinois, by the name of "GALENA COMMANDERY,"
AND WHEREAS, Application has been made to this Grand Commandery for a perpetual Charter or Warrant, to enable them to continue in all the rights and privileges of a regularly constituted Commandery, and a copy of the By-Laws, and of the Minutes of their proceedings having been submitted for our inspection and approval, and no cause adverse to the granting the prayer of said applicants to us appearing;
NOW KNOW YE, That we, the Grand Commandery of Knights Templar of the State of Illinois, reposing special confidence and trust in the fidelity, zeal, and Knightly courtesy of the officers and Knights of the said Commandery, and for the purpose of diffusing the benefits of the Order, and promoting the happiness of man, by virtue of the power in us vested ; Do by these presents, recognize said Commandery to be known as "GALENA COMMANDERY No, 40," as regularly constituted and established under the jurisdiction of this Grand Commandery with full and adequate powers to confer the several Orders of Knights of the Red Cross, Knights Templar and Knights of Malta, upon such person or persons posessing the requisite qualifications, as they may think proper. And we do also recognize the present Officers and Knights of the said Commandery, with continuence of the same powers and privileges to them and their successors forever, except that the Officers of said Commandery shall not be entitled to act as members of our Grand Commandery, until they are duly elected and installed under this Charter; *Provided*, Nevertheless, that the said Officers and Knights, and their successors pay due respect to our said Grand Commandery, the Statutes and Regulations thereof, and the constitution and edicts of the Grand Encampment of the United States of America; and in no way remove the ancient land-marks of our order, otherwise this Charter, and all things therein conatined to be void and of no effect.
Given at Chicago, in the State of Illinois, this twenty-second day of December, in the year of our Lord one thousand eight hundred and seventy-one, and of the order, seven hundred and fifty-three.
!Signed.

WILEY M. EGAN, Grand Com,
DANIEL DUSTIN, Dep. Grand Com.
JAMES A. HAWLEY, Grand Generalissimo.
HIRAM W. HUBBARD, Grand Capt. Gen.
[SEAL]   JAMES H, MILES, Grand Recorder.

BY-LAWS.

ARTICLE I.

NAME.

The name of this Commandery shall be "GALENA COMMANDERY, No. 40," under the jurisdiction of the Grand Commandery of Illinois.

ARTICLE II.

STATED CONCLAVES.

The stated conclaves of this Commandery shall be held on the first Thursday of each month at 7½ o clock, P. M.

ARTICLE III.

ANNUAL CONCLAVES.

The Annual Conclave for the election of Officers shall be held on the first Thursday of December of each year.

ARTICLE IV.

ELECTION OF OFFICERS,

The Eminent Commander, Generalissimo, Captain General, Prelate, Senior Warden, Junior Warden, Treasurer, Recorder, Standard Bearer, Sword Bearer, and Warden shall be elected by ballot, at the annual Conclave of each year.

ARTICLE V.

OFFICERS APPOINTED.

Previous to the Installation, the Eminent Commander-elect shall appoint a Captain of the Guards, three Guards and two Stewards.

ARTICLE VI.

INSTALLATION OF OFFICERS.

The Installation of Officers shall occur as soon after the election as may be convenient, but on or before Saint John's day, December 27th of each year.

ARTICLE VII.

DUTIES OF OFFICERS.

The duties of the several Officers shall be in accordance with the work and ritual of the Order, the traditions, statutes, and regulations of the Grand Commandery of the State, and the Constitution of the Grand Encampment of the United States of America.

ARTICLE VIII.

BOND OF TREASURER.

Before entering upon the duties of his office, the Treasurer shall give good and sufficient surety for the faithful performance and discharge of his duty, to be approved by the first three Officers-elect.

ARTICLE IX.

ANNUAL REPORTS OF SECRETARY AND TREASURER.

At each annual conclave, the Treasurer and Recorder shall render an account of all moneys received and paid out by them respectively, for the current year, which accounts shall be examined by the Finance Committee, who shall report the result of their examinations to the Commandery, and proper action shall be had thereon.

ARTICLE X.

FINANCE COMMITTEE.

The Eminent Commander, Generalissimo, and Captain-General shall be a Committee on Finance, and all bills shall be referred to and audited by them.

ARTICLE XI.

ANNUAL DUES.

The yearly dues of members shall be three dollars (which includes the Grand Commandery dues) payable on or before the annual conclave in each year.

ARTICLE XII.

LIFE MEMBERSHIP.

SEC. 1. Any member of this Commandery not indebted for dues or otherwise, may become a life member of this Commandery and exempt from the payment of further dues, by paying into the Treasury thereof the sum of thirty dollars, and thereby remain and be entitled to all the rights and privileges of active membership.

SEC. 2. Any member of this Commandery who has regularly paid all dues and assessments against him for twenty years, shall become a life member and be exempt from the payment of all further dues, and be entitled to all the rights and privileges of active membership.

SEC. 3. Any Sir Knight becoming a life member,

as provided in Section 1 and 2, shall remain as before, subject to all the laws, rules and edicts of the Order, and its ancient landmarks, usages and constitutions; and in case of expulsion shall forfeit the sum so paid for life membership, and all the privileges of said iife membership.

ARTICLE XIII.
RECORDER AND CAPTAIN OF GUARD.

The Recorder and Captain of the Guard shall be exempt from the payment of yearly dues, and shall each receive cne dollar for each night's services.

ARTICLE XIV.
INDEBTEDENESS FOR DUES.

It shall be the duty of the Recorder at each Annual Conclave, to read the names in open Commandery, of any members who shall be in arrears for due, for one year or over, and any member so in arrears shall not be entitled to vote at the Annual Conclaves or be eligible to office, and such action shall be had in such cases as may be directed by a majority of the members present.

ARTICLE XV.
FEES FOR ORDERS.

The Fees for conferring the orders shall be forty dollars, viz: Twenty dollars for the Order of the Red Cross (ten dollars of which shall accompany the petition) and twenty dollars for the Order of Knights Templar, and Knight of Malta, which amounts shall be paid at or before the time of conferring the several orders. The Fee for membership of a Knight

Templar shall be five dollars, which shall accompany the petition, and in case of the rejection of a petitioner for the orders, or for membership, the Recorder shall at once return said fee to such petitioner with a notice of his rejection.

ARTICLE XVI.

PETITIONS.

Every petition for the orders or for membership, shall be recommend by two members of this Commandery in good standing, and a unanimous ballot shall be necessary to elect.

ARTICLE XVII.

FAILURE OF CANDIDATE TO APPEAR.

A Candidate elect failing to appear to receive the Orders within six months after being notified in writing of his election, shall be required to present a new petition to be acted upon, and the fee accompanying the first shall be forfeited to the Commandery.

ARTICLE XVIII.

DEMITS.

A Demit may be granted to any member (excepting Officers) in good standing, and clear of the books, on his application, at a stated Conclave.

ARTICLE XIX.

DRESS AND UNIFORM.

Every member attending the stated Conclaves shall be dressed uniformly in dark, and in case of failure or neglect to provide himself with the Regulation Uniform of a Knight Templar within three months after his membership shall commence, he shall not be

allowed to appear in public with the Commandery,
and such failure or neglect may, in the discretion of
the Commandery, be sufficient cause for the suspension of the delinquent member from the rights and
privileges of the order.

ARTICLE XX.

CHARGES.

Whenever charges unbecoming a Knight Templar
shall be preferred against a member, such action shall
be had, as is consistent with the traditions and rules of
the order, and in conformity with the statutes and
regulations of the Grand Comandery of the State,
and the Constitution of the Grand Encampment of
the United States of America.

ARTICLE XXI.

AMENDMENTS TO BY-LAWS.

Any proposed amendment to these By-Laws shall
be presented in writing at a stated Conclave, and
lie over until the next stated Conclave, when action
shall be had thereon; a two-thirds vote of all members present shall be necessary to the adoption of any
such amendment.

ORDER OF BUSINESS.

The order of Business shall be as follows:
1. Reading of Records.
2. Reading and referring Petitions·
3. Reports of Committees on Petitions.
4. Belloting on Petitions.
5. Miscellaneous Business.
5. Work.

UNIFORM

ADOPTED BY THE

Grand Commandery of Knights Templar,

OF THE STATE OF ILLINOIS.

OCTOBER 24, 1870.

Conforming to that adopted by the Grand Encampment of the United States.

Full Dress—Black frock coat, black pantaloons, scarf, sword, belt, shoulder straps, gauntlets, and chapeau, with appropriate trimmings.

COAT.

For Sir Knights,—Black cloth cut military style, single breasted, standing collar; eleven buttons in front, four behind; length, to knee; side edges in plait; hook and eye at neck gore, sleeve plain, no buttons at cuff; passion cross of silver on left side of collar, buttons round or bell, and of silk twisted covering.

For Generalissimo and Captain General.—Same as above.

For Commanders and Past Commander.—Same as above, except that the coat shall be double breasted, with two rows of buttons; cross on collar to be gold with rays. *

Fatigue Dress.—Same as full dress, except for chapeau a black cloth cap, navy form, with appropriate cross in front, an l for gauntlets white gloves.

Scars.—Five inches wide in the whole, of white, bordered with black one inch on either side, a strip of navy lace one-fourth of an inch wide, at the inner edge of the black. On the front centre of the scarf, a metal star of nine points, in allusion to the nine founders of the Temple Order, inclosing the Passion Cross, surrounded by the Latin motto, "*In hoc Signo Vinces*," the star to be three and three-quarter inches in diameter. The scarf to be worn from the right shoulder to the left hip, with the ends extending six inches below the point of intersection.

Chapeau.—The military chapeau, trimmed with black binding, one white and two black plumes, and appropriate cross an the left side.

Gauntlets.—Of buff leather, the flap to extend four inches upwards from the wrist, and to have the appropriate cross embroidered in gold, on the proper colored velvet, two inches in length.

Sword.—Thirty-four to forty inches, inclusive of scabbard, helmit head, cross handle, and metal scabbard.

---

* None but Commanders and Past Commanders are entitled to use the rays.

Belt.—Red enamled or patent leather, two inches wide, fastened around the body with buckle or clasp.

Shoulder Straps, for the Commander and Past Commanders of a Subordinate Commandery—Emerald green silk velvet, one and a half inches wide by four inches long, bordered with one row of embroidery, of gold, quarter of an inch wide; the Passion Cross with a halo, embroidered, of silver, in the centre.

For the Generalissimo.—Same as Commander, except for Passion Cross, the Square, surmounted with the Paschal Lamb.

For the Captain General.—Same as the Commander, except for the Passion Cross, the level, surmounted with the Cock.

Cap.—Navy form; black cloth, four to five inches high, narrow leather strap fastened at the sides with small metal Templar's Cross, and with appropriate cross in front.

Distinctions.—The Sir Knights will wear white metal wherever metal appears. Commanders and Past Commanders, Grand and Past Grand Officers, gold.

Officers U. D.

A. O. 753; A. D. 1871.

E. Sir John Corson Smith,   Eminent Com.
Sir Samuel Cook,   Generalissimo.
Sir Simeon Kingsley Miner,   Captain General.
Sir John Minot Daggett,   Prelate.
Sir Mortimer Marcus Wheeler, Senior Warden.
Sir John Olinger,   Junior Warden.
Sir Charles Silas Burt,   Treasurer.
Sir Daniel LeBetter,   Recorder.
Sir Robert Little,   Standard Bearer.
Sir Smith D. Atkins,   Sword Bearer.
Sir Daniel Stewart,   Captain of Guards.

Officers.

A. O. 754; A. D. 1872

———◆◆◆———

E. Sir John Corson Smith,	Eminent Com.
Sir William Reuben Rowley,	Generalissimo.
Sir Simeon Kingsley Miner,	Captain General.
Sir Daniel LeBetter,	Prelate.
Sir Mahlon Coleman,	Senior Warden.
Sir Mortimer Marcus Wheeler,	Junior Warden.
Sir William Rudolph Burkhard,	Treasurer.
Sir Daniel LeBetter,	Recorder.
Sir Richard Henry Fiddick,	Standard Bearer.
Sir Edward James,	Sword Bearer.
Sir John Carter Calderwood,	Warder.
Sir Daniel Stewart,	Captain of Guard.
Sir Sidney Hunkins,	Third Guard.
Sir William Richard Holder,	Second Guard.
Sir Charles Sherman Bentley,	First Guard.

Officers.

A. O. 755; A. D. 1873.

E. Sir John Corson Smith,	Eminent Com.
Sir William Reuben Rowley,	Generalissimo.
Sir Charles Sherman Bentley,	Captain General.
Sir Henry Herman Oldenhage,	Prelate.
Sir Mahlon Coleman,	Senior Warden.
Sir Simeon Kingsley Miner,	Junior Warden.
Sir Richard Henry Fiddick,	Treasurer.
Sir Daniel LeBetter,	Recorder.
Sir Edward James,	Standard Bearer.
Sir Louis Albert Rowley,	Sword Bearer.
Sir John Carter Calderwood,	Warden.
Sir Daniel Stewart,	Captain of Guard.
Sir Thomas Edmond Armitstead,	Third Guard.
Sir Sidney Hunkins,	Second Guard.
Sir William Richard Holder.	First Guard.

SIR KNIGHTS AT DATE OF CONSTITUTING COMMANDERY, AND CREATED SINCE ORGANIZATION.

§ Demitted.   ‡ Honorary.   † Deceased.

MEMBERS ON DISPENSATION.

E. Sir John Corson Smith,   ∠
Sir Samuel Cook, †
Sir Simeon Kingsley Miner,
Sir John Minott Daggett, §
Sir Mortimer Marcus Wheeler,
Sir John Olinger, §
Sir Charles Silas Burt, §
Sir Robert Little, §
Sir Smith D. Atkins, §   ✓·

		When Knighted.
Sir Kt. John Corson Smith,	April	26, 1871
" Simeon Kingsley Miner,	April	26, 1871
" Mortimer Marcus Wheeler,	April	5, 1870
" William Reuben Rowley,	Sept.	29, 1871
" Daniel Stewart,	Sept.	29, 1871
" Mahlon Coleman,	Sept.	29, 1871
" Daniel LeBetter,	Sept.	29, 1871
" John Carter Calderwood,	Sept.	29, 1871
" William Rudolph Burkhard, §	Sept.	29, 1871
" Edward James, ·	Jan.	12, 1872
" Richard Henry Fiddick,	Jan.	13, 1872

Sir Kt. Charles Sherman Bentley,	Feb.	3,	1872
" Nelson Munroe Bratt,	Feb.	7,	1872
" Amasa Harrington Moody,	Feb.	7,	1872
" Hezekiah Gear, ‡	March	8,	1872
" William Richard Holder,	March	22,	1872
" Daniel Wann,	March	22,	1872
" Jacob Wernli,	May	10,	1872
" Sidney Hunkins,	May	11,	1872
" Henry Herman Oldenhage,	May	13,	1872
" William Henry Martin,	May	14,	1872
" Wilbur Fisk Crummer,	May	15,	1872
" Louis Albert Rowley,	June	17,	1872
" William Cary,	June	17,	1872
" Thomas Edmond Armitstead §	June	19,	1872
" John Dunston Pryor, §	Nov.	29,	1872
" Elijah Hedding Downing, ‡	Jan.	27,	1873
" John Wesley Luke,	Jan.	29,	1873
" Peter Trewartha,	Jan.	31,	1873
" James Barton Brown,	Feb.	24,	1873
" Daniel Asbury Taylor,	March	20,	1873
" Alonzo Van Ness Richards,	April	12,	1873
" Jacob Fawcett,	April	17,	1873
" Edward Courtney,	May	10,	1873
" Benjamin Frederic Merten,	May	12,	1873
" John Hatch,	July	25,	1873
" John Paul Williams,	Aug.	21,	1873
" John Eugene Hoover,	Aug.	27,	1873
" John Stewart Wiley,	Aug.	27,	1873
" David Nash Corwith,	Dec.	12,	1873
" Horatio Nelson Bridgeman,	Dec.	12,	1873